LUCENT LIBRARY OF
BLACK HISTORY

REPARATIONS FOR SLAVERY

The Fight for Compensation

By Sarah Goldy-Brown

Portions of this book originally appeared in *Reparations for Slavery* by Cherese Cartlidge.

LUCENT
PRESS

Published in 2018 by
Lucent Press, an Imprint of Greenhaven Publishing, LLC
353 3rd Avenue
Suite 255
New York, NY 10010

Designer: Deanna Paternostro
Editor: Jessica Moore

Library of Congress Cataloging-in-Publication Data

Names: Goldy-Brown, Sarah, author.
Title: Reparations for slavery : the fight for compensation / Sarah Goldy-Brown.
Description: New York : Lucent Press, 2018. | Series: Lucent library of Black history | Includes bibliographical references and index.
Identifiers: LCCN 2017049212| ISBN 9781534562332 (library bound book) | ISBN 9781534562974 (pbk. book) | ISBN 9781534562349 (ebook)
Subjects: LCSH: African Americans–Reparations. | Slavery–United States–History.
Classification: LCC E185.89.R45 G65 2018 | DDC 306.3/620973–dc23
LC record available at https://lccn.loc.gov/2017049212

Printed in the United States of America

CPSIA compliance information: Batch #CW18KL: For further information contact Greenhaven Publishing LLC, New York, New York at 1-844-317-7404.

Please visit our website, www.greenhavenpublishing.com. For a free color catalog of all our high-quality books, call toll free 1-844-317-7404 or fax 1-844-317-7405.

CONTENTS

FOREWORD

Black men and women in the United States have become successful in every field, but they have faced incredible challenges while striving for that success. They have overcome racial barriers, violent prejudice, and hostility on every side, all while continuing to advance technology, literature, the arts, and much more.

From medicine and law to sports and literature, African Americans have come to excel in every industry. However, the story of African Americans has often been one of prejudice and persecution. More than 300 years ago, Africans were taken in chains from their home and enslaved to work for the earliest American settlers. They suffered for more than two centuries under the brutal oppression of their owners, until the outbreak of the American Civil War in 1861. After the dust settled four years later and thousands of Americans—both black and white—had died in combat, slavery in the United States had been legally abolished. By the turn of the 20th century, with the help of the 13th, 14th, and 15th Amendments to the U.S. Constitution, African American men had finally won significant battles for the basic rights of citizenship. Then, with the passage of the groundbreaking Civil Rights Act of 1964, many people of all races began to believe that America was finally ready to start moving toward a more equal future.

These triumphs of human equality were achieved with help from brave social activists such as Frederick Douglass, Martin Luther King Jr., and Maya Angelou. They all experienced racial prejudice in their lifetimes and fought by writing, speaking, and peacefully acting against it. By exposing the suffering of the black community, they brought the United States together to try and remedy centuries' worth of wrongdoing. Today, it is important to learn about the history of African Americans and their experiences in modern America in order to work toward healing the divide that still exists in the United States. This series aims to give readers a deeper appreciation for and understanding of a part of the American story that is often left untold.

Even before the legal emancipation of slaves, black culture was thriving despite many attempts to suppress it. From the 1600s to the 1800s, slaves developed their own cultural perspective. From music, to language, to art, slaves began cultivating an identity that was completely unique. Soon after these slaves were granted citizenship and were integrated into American society, African American culture burst into the mainstream. New generations of authors, scholars, painters, and singers were born, and they spread an appreciation for black culture across America and the entire world. Studying the contributions of these talented individuals fosters a sense of optimism. Despite the cruel treatment and racist attitudes they faced, these men and women never gave up, changing the world with their determination and unique voice. Discovering the triumphs and tragedies of the oppressed allows readers to gain a clearer picture of American history and American cultural identity.

Here to help young readers with this discovery, this series offers a glimpse into the lives and accomplishments of some of the most important and influential African Americans across historical time periods. Titles examine primary source documents and quotes from contemporary thinkers and observers to provide a full and nuanced learning experience for readers. With thoroughly researched text, unique sidebars, and a carefully selected bibliography for further research, this series is an invaluable resource for young scholars. Moreover, it does not shy away from reconciling the brutality of the past with a sense of hopefulness for the future. This series provides critical tools for understanding more about how black history is a vital part of American history.

SETTING THE SCENE:

1619
Twenty captured Africans land at Jamestown, Virginia, becoming the first Africans in the British colonies.

1865
The American Civil War ends, and the 13th Amendment is passed, abolishing slavery. Three years later, the 14th Amendment grants full U.S. citizenship to African Americans.

1619 1863 1865 1875 1896

1863
The Emancipation Proclamation goes into effect, freeing slaves in the Confederate states.

1896
The U.S. Supreme Court rules in *Plessy v. Ferguson* that separate but equal facilities for blacks and whites are constitutional.

1875
The Civil Rights Act of 1875 bars segregation in public places; it was declared unconstitutional eight years later.

A TIMELINE

1954
In *Brown v. Board of Education*, the U.S. Supreme Court reverses its earlier decision in *Plessy v. Ferguson* and bans segregated schools.

2008
Barack Obama becomes the first African American to be elected U.S. president, suggesting a shift in American politics.

2016
The United Nations formally recommends that the United States begin slavery reparations efforts by passing H.R. 40.

1954 | 1989 | 2002 | 2007 | 2008 | 2009 | 2016

1989
Representative John Conyers Jr. of Michigan introduces H.R. 40, a proposal for a commission to study reparations for slavery; he continues to introduce it every year.

2002
Activist Deidra Farmer-Paellmann files a class-action lawsuit in federal court on behalf of 35 million African Americans.

2009
Concurrent resolution 26 is passed by the Senate, apologizing for slavery and the Jim Crow laws.

2007
Virginia becomes the first U.S. state to issue a public apology for its role in slavery. North Carolina, Alabama, New Jersey, Florida, Tennessee, and Connecticut do the same over the next two years.

INTRODUCTION

SLAVERY'S EFFECT ON AMERICA

From the time of its founding, the United States has struggled with race relations. Poor race relations between black and white Americans began because slavery based on race was legal in parts of the United States until 1865. During the period of legal slavery, black Americans were seen in many places as inferior to white Americans and had no legal rights whatsoever. It has been more than 150 years since slavery was abolished and more than 50 years since segregation based on race was outlawed in the United States, but the long history of slavery and racial discrimination in America continues to affect the everyday lives of both black and white Americans.

Despite their success, former President Barack Obama and former First Lady Michelle Obama are not immune to racism, as some might suggest. Both recalled situations where others mistook them for "the help" or valets simply because of their skin color. As president, Obama faced animosity for factors outside of his control. During his presidential campaign and throughout his presidency, many Americans questioned his citizenship status and demanded proof that he was born in the United States. Some felt he came across as a foreigner because his father was a black Kenyan and his mother a white American. This issue arose solely because of his ethnicity and race.

Like the Obamas, Molefi Kete Asante, a professor of African American studies at Temple University, has witnessed racism firsthand. Asante described everyday racial discrimination experienced by African Americans in the United States:

We walk into an automobile showroom and we are quoted

Barack and Michelle Obama entered the White House in 2009, making him the first black president and her the first black first lady.

higher prices than whites; we work as cooks in restaurants where whites with less skill and less time in the job are paid more; we step into employment agencies and they direct us away from jobs, high school guidance counselors direct us away from college ... We are told that there are no apartments available, but when our white friends call the same agency they are told there are several apartments available.[1]

Statistics show that conditions for black Americans today are quite different from those for white Americans. As of 2015, the median income of black individuals is only 59.5 percent that of white individuals. The median income of black Americans is $36,544 each year, while white Americans earn $61,394. According to data from the U.S. Census Bureau in 2016, 24.1 percent of black individuals live in poverty, compared to only 11.6 percent of white individuals. While 29.3 percent of non-Hispanic white Americans have a bachelor's degree or higher, only 17.7 percent of black Americans do. Black college graduates also face an unemployment rate nearly twice as high as that of their white peers. The infant mortality rate for black Americans is more than twice that for non-Latinx white Americans, and black Americans have a lower life expectancy rate than their white counterparts. The fact that black individuals comprise only 13.3 percent of the U.S. population but account for 59.7 percent of the prison population as of 2010 points to a particularly glaring disparity between races.

John David Smith, a distinguished history professor, described the prevalence of racism in the United States today: "Racism continues to stain the fabric of American society … Subtle, and not so subtle, acts of segregation, racial injustice, and racial violence are common in education, housing, government, law, business, and the arts. Racism and intolerance lurk in the corners of American culture like an incurable social cancer."[2]

Others feel differently. Even though major race-related riots continue to happen in the United States, many Americans still believe that racism is no longer prevalent in the United

The Black Lives Matter movement began in 2013 in response to acts of violence against unarmed African Americans.

INVISIBLE TO MANY

In his award-winning, semi-autobiographical novel *Invisible Man*, written in the mid-20th century, Ralph Ellison depicts racial problems in the United States and explores the experience many black Americans face of being ignored or overlooked. In the prologue, he describes a phenomenon that many African Americans still experience today:

> *I am an invisible man. No, I am not a spook like those who haunted Edgar Allan Poe; nor am I one of your Hollywood-movie ectoplasms. I am a man of substance, of flesh and bone, fiber and liquids—and I might even be said to possess a mind. I am invisible understand, simply because people refuse to see me ... When they approach me they see only my surroundings, themselves, or figments of their imagination—indeed, everything and anything except me.*[1]

Ralph Ellison published Invisible Man *in 1952, and it holds spot number 19 on Modern Library's 100 Best Novels list.*

1. Ralph Ellison, *Invisible Man*. New York, NY: Vintage International, 1995, e-book.

States. Many feel that discrimination based on someone's skin color stopped in the 1960s, during the civil rights movement. A 2014 study suggests that others believe racial discrimination ended in 2008 with the election of President Obama. Many individuals studied think that his success and that of other prominent African Americans proves that systemic racial barriers to success no longer exist. It is obvious to many others, especially people of color, that African Americans still face bigotry and discrimination.

President Obama spoke to this idea during a podcast interview in 2015:

> *What is true is that the legacy of slavery, Jim Crow, discrimination in almost every institution of our lives—you know, that casts a long shadow. And that's still part of our DNA that's passed on … Societies don't overnight completely erase everything that happened 200–300 years prior.*[3]

Roy L. Brooks, a law professor who has written extensively on race relations, perhaps summed it up best when he said, "The legacy of the past impinges on the present."[4]

It is no wonder then that many people, both black and white Americans, have joined the movement to obtain reparations for slavery in the United States.

While the concept of reparations for slavery is supported by many, it remains a highly controversial idea. As a result, most efforts to obtain reparations for former slaves and their descendants have been unsuccessful.

CHAPTER ONE
DEFINING SLAVERY REPARATIONS

Reparations are a way to make amends for past wrongdoing in the form of an apology, money, or other measures. Individuals and organizations have sought reparations from the U.S. government since slavery's abolishment in the 1860s. Slave traders and owners forced millions of Africans to work in an unfamiliar land where no one spoke their language. These slaves were stolen from their families, deprived of their culture, abused, and never paid for their work. The majority of Americans agree that these acts were immoral and despicable, yet a formal apology or plan for compensation has never been made.

A Brief History of Reparations

The word "reparations" shares the same Latin ancestor and has a similar meaning as the word "repair." Both words have to do with restoring or fixing something that has been injured or damaged. Reparations carries with it the idea of making amends for a wrong that has been committed. They are often made in the form of monetary payments but can include an apology, an admission of wrongdoing, a return of lands, or special programs to help the harmed party. In the 20th century, the defeated nation of Germany was required to make reparations after both world wars to the victorious Allied nations. Furthermore, Germany was required to accept sole responsibility for causing World War I.

Reparations are not just made by nations defeated in war. Many groups around the world have received reparations for crimes committed against them, including Australian aborigines, New Zealand Maoris, and Jewish victims of the Holocaust. In the United States, Alaska natives and several Native American tribes have been paid

WHAT AMERICA OWES TO BLACKS

In his book *The Debt: What America Owes to Blacks*, Randall Robinson explains that demanding restitution for slavery would help African Americans gain a measure of self-awareness of their past as well as the damage done to them by the long history of enslavement:

> *We would also show ourselves to be responding as any normal people would to victimization were we to assert collectively in our demands for restitution that, for 246 years and with the complicity of the United States government, hundreds of millions of black people endured unimaginable cruelties—kidnapping, sale as livestock, deaths in the millions during terror-filled sea voyages, backbreaking toil, beatings, rapes, castrations, maimings, murders. We would begin a healing of our psyches were the most public case made that whole peoples lost religions, languages, customs, histories, cultures, children, mothers, fathers. It would make us more forgiving of ourselves, more self-approving, more self-understanding to see, really see, that on three continents and a string of islands, survivors had little choice but to piece together whole new cultures from the rubble shards ... And they were never made whole. And never compensated. Not one red cent.*[1]

1. Randall Robinson, *The Debt: What America Owes to Blacks*. New York, NY: Dutton, 2000, p. 208.

millions of dollars in compensation for treaty violations, and some even had their land returned to them. In 1993, Native Hawaiians received a formal apology from President Bill Clinton for the way in which the United States took over their nation in the late 19th century. Japanese Americans who were held in internment camps during World War II also received an official apology and monetary reparations in the amount of $20,000 each from the U.S. government.

One organization that seeks similar

reparations for African Americans is the National Coalition of Blacks for Reparations in America (N'COBRA). On its website, N'COBRA states,

> *Reparations is a process of repairing, healing and restoring a people injured because of their group identity and in violation of their fundamental human rights by governments or corporations. Those groups that have been injured have the right to obtain from the government or corporation responsible for the injuries that which they need to repair and heal themselves. In addition to being a demand for justice, it is a principle of international human rights law.*[5]

The current U.S. slave reparations movement stems not only from the conditions of American slavery but also from the continuing effects of centuries of racial discrimination that began with slavery.

Slavery Based Solely on Race

Slavery existed throughout the world long before the American colonies were formed. However, slavery as practiced in the Americas introduced a new element—that of race. Throughout history, slaves generally belonged to the same race as their masters, but in the colonies, Brooks said, "for the first time in history, dark skin became the social marker of chattel slavery."[6] This view of blacks as inferior to whites, which was used to justify enslaving Africans, persisted in American society long after slavery was abolished. For some, this view of black inferiority is still held today. Brooks explained the widespread and enduring effects of racially based slavery on African Americans:

> *For the first time in Western civilization, the slaves took serious note of the fact that master and slave were of different races. More than that, slavers targeted dark-skinned people and, not coincidentally, developed a racist ideology that sought to justify this practice—a social marker that affected free blacks as well and that continues to outlive slavery itself.*[7]

In addition to being based on race, the institution of slavery in the American colonies and the newly formed United States was particularly harmful and brutal. Moreover, for the first time in history, humans were being transported in massive numbers thousands of miles across an ocean to be sold into bondage in an unfamiliar land.

The Slave Trade

In 1619, 20 African indentured servants became the first blacks to set foot in the British North American colonies when they landed at Jamestown, Virginia. They were not slaves, however, because indentured servants could eventually gain their freedom. By 1641, the Massachusetts Bay Colony introduced slavery, making Africans a slaveholder's legal property with no chance of earning freedom. Other colonies soon did the same. It is impossible to know the exact number of people who were enslaved in the United States because accurate records were not kept. By 1781, there were approximately 575,000 men, women, and children held in slavery in the United States; by the outbreak of the American Civil War, 80 years later, that number had grown to 4 million.

In Africa, people captured in war or kidnapped by neighboring groups were marched in chains to the coast to be sold to European and American slave traders. This was just the first stage of the transatlantic slave trade. Up to half of the captives did not survive the long march. Those who did faced a voyage across the Atlantic Ocean in severely overcrowded ships. Known as the Middle Passage, this voyage could take anywhere from three to ten weeks. Aboard the ships, humans were packed

After crossing the Atlantic on ships from Africa, slaves were sold throughout America's southern states at slave auctions.

so tightly below deck at night that they could hardly move around at all. Some ship captains allowed the captives to come above the deck during the day, but others did not. This meant that some people spent the entire voyage confined to a cramped deck that was only 4 to 5 feet (1.2 to 1.5 m) high.

Life aboard the slave ships was miserable. Not only were slaves regularly beaten and kept in chains, but exercise, food, and sanitary facilities were inadequate. Slaves were generally fed only two meals a day, which typically consisted of a bland, unchanging diet of corn, rice, yams, or perhaps beans.

Shown here is one African American family whose members were all born on the same southern plantation.

Food and water often became contaminated, but the slaves consumed it anyway because there was nothing else to eat or drink. Diseases such as dysentery were rampant on these ships. The tight quarters, lack of sunlight, and large amount of people created extremely unsanitary conditions. Men, women, and children aboard the slave ships also suffered from profound fear, anxiety, and depression. Those who could not handle the horrors sometimes committed suicide by jumping overboard or simply refusing to eat.

It is estimated that 10 to 16 percent of the people shipped across the Atlantic perished aboard the slave ships. If they managed to survive the Middle Passage, they were then sold on an auction block like livestock. Those who bought slaves included ordinary people, farmers, and even U.S. presidents. Even though the United States prohibited the further importation of slaves in 1808, slavery was still legal and continued to exist in the new nation as generation after generation of African Americans were born into bondage.

Three-Fifths of a Person

Conditions for Africans enslaved in the United States were horrific. Slaves were seen as their masters' property and had no legal rights. Their clothing, housing, diet, and medical care were inadequate, and they suffered from malnutrition and disease. Field slaves often worked long hours performing hard physical labor in harsh climates. Slaves who worked in their masters' houses were generally better treated, but many slaves were subjected to harsh, cruel punishments, including whipping, maiming, and even castration. If a slave escaped, he or she was hunted down and severely punished if caught. Slave owners even had the legal right to put an uncooperative or rebellious slave to death.

The legal status of slaves and free blacks in the United States was officially defined by the Supreme Court when Dred Scott, a slave, sued for his freedom and that of his wife and children. In its 1857 decision in the case of *Dred Scott v. Sanford*, the Supreme Court declared that black slaves were not U.S. citizens and furthermore, defined them as "beings of an inferior order, and altogether unfit to associate with the white race, either in social or political relations; and so far inferior that they had no rights which the white man was bound to respect."[8] In fact, the 1787 Constitutional Convention created what is known as the Three-Fifths Compromise, which determined that each slave counted as only three-fifths of a person for

Dred Scott's lawsuit forced the U.S. judicial system to officially rule on whether or not slaves were U.S. citizens.

purposes of determining population and political representation.

Slaves had no rights at all. Many were married, but their marriages were not recognized as legal. Husbands could be sold away from wives, and children could be sold away from parents. There were even laws that made it illegal for a slave to learn to read or for anyone to attempt to educate a slave. An 1831 Mississippi law forbade any black person, free or slave, to preach from the Bible; violators were to receive 39 lashes with a whip.

Asante explained how the institution of slavery affected African Americans:

> *To deny freedom, will, culture, religion, and health is to create the most thorough conditions for loss. The Africans who were enslaved in America were among the most deprived humans in history.*[9]

Free but Not Really Free

After the Civil War, the 13th Amendment to the U.S. Constitution formally abolished slavery. For African Americans who had been deprived of even the most basic rights, freedom represented challenges. Most had nothing when they were freed. They were uneducated and without jobs, homes, or land. Many former slaves were no better off than they had been during slavery.

Slavery was replaced by a system of sharecropping, in which former slaves continued to work on their masters' lands for a share of the profits. White

Each year on April 16, citizens of Washington, D.C., celebrate Emancipation Day, an official holiday commemorating the anniversary of the abolishment of slavery in Washington, D.C.

landowners often cheated the former slaves out of fair wages. A similar system was known as peonage, or convict labor. Under peonage, people who were incarcerated could be leased out to work on farms or in chain gangs to build roads. Under sharecropping and peonage, many freed slaves continued to live in conditions of extreme poverty and near-slavery, as Yuval Taylor explained in the book *I Was Born a Slave*:

> *Although they were not called* slavery, *the ... practices of peonage, forced convict labor, and to a lesser degree share-cropping essentially continued the institution of slavery well into the twentieth century, and were in some ways even worse. Peonage, for example, was a complex system in which a black man would be arrested for "vagrancy," another word for unemployment, ordered to pay a fine he could not afford, and incarcerated. A plantation owner would pay his fine and "hire" him until he could afford to pay off the fine himself: The peon was then forced to work, locked up at night, and, if he ran away, chased by bloodhounds until recaptured.*[10]

In fact, there is evidence that, although illegal, slavery actually continued in a modified form up until the 1950s. For example, in the 1920s and 1930s, investigations by the National Association for the Advancement of Colored People (NAACP) found several instances of African Americans who were being forced to work on farms without pay. Since slavery was illegal at this time, the landowners were prosecuted and sentenced to prison. In 1954, two white men, the Dial brothers, were prosecuted for holding two black men in involuntary servitude on their farm in Sumpter County, Alabama. One of the black men attempted to escape from the farm but was captured and severely beaten. He died three days later. The Dial brothers received prison sentences in what writer Len Cooper referred to as "one of the last slavery convictions in the United States."[11]

Reconstruction to the Jim Crow Era

The Civil War was followed by the Reconstruction period, during which the South began to rebuild and the nation attempted to reunite. During Reconstruction, which lasted from 1865 to 1877, African Americans made several significant civil rights gains. The 14th Amendment granted them citizenship rights and equal protection of the law, and the 15th Amendment gave black males the right to vote. The Civil Rights Act of 1866 granted all citizens, black and white, equal rights to enter into contracts; sue; testify in court; and inherit, purchase, and sell property. During Reconstruction, 22 African Americans were elected to Congress.

However, the successes of the Reconstruction period were short-lived, as many white individuals, particularly in the South, felt threatened by former slaves who were exercising their newfound freedoms. Reconstruction gave way to a period known as the Jim Crow era, which lasted until the 1960s. During this time, Southern states passed laws that restricted the equality and voting rights of African Americans and prohibited black and white individuals from mingling in virtually every way. Black and white individuals had to use separate stores, post offices, public transportation, libraries, drinking fountains, hospitals, public parks, schools, and cemeteries. Marriages between the races were prohibited in all Southern states. In 1896, the U.S. Supreme Court decided in the case of *Plessy v. Ferguson* that separating

During the time of segregation, black and white Americans had separate seats on the bus, bathrooms, waiting rooms, schools, and water fountains.

EFFECTS OF SUBTLE DISCRIMINATION

African Americans were terrorized by violence in the form of lynchings throughout the late 19th century and the 20th century. Racial discrimination also happened in more subtle, but equally harmful, ways. Writer Sarah Bracey White recalls growing up in the segregated South in the 1950s when black individuals were still paid less than white individuals for doing the exact same job. She described the effect this had on her family:

> *Our long-absent father had once challenged the fairness of paying colored teachers less than white teachers and joined the National Association for the Advancement of Colored People to seek equal pay. He was fired from his principal's job and blacklisted from teaching. Our family lost everything, and he started drinking heavily, then drifted away.*[1]

1. Quoted in Laurel Holliday, *Dreaming in Color, Living in Black and White: Our Own Stories of Growing Up Black in America*. New York, NY: Archway, 2000, p. 43.

the two races was legal as long as public facilities, such as schools, were equal for all races. In reality, facilities for black individuals were often poorly funded and inferior to those of white individuals, but this was difficult to prove in court.

The racially repressive state laws of the Jim Crow era, as well as the Supreme Court decision in the *Plessy v. Ferguson* case, meant that discrimination against African Americans in the United States was officially sanctioned by the government. African Americans were discriminated against in hiring practices, housing policies, and the courts.

One of the most heinous effects of slavery and the century of discrimination that followed was the violence perpetrated against African Americans, often in the form of lynching. Lynching is the brutal murder of a person, generally carried out by a mob. Lynching of African Americans was common throughout the South

In 1896, Justice John M. Harland was the only justice on the U.S. Supreme Court to disagree with the Plessy v. Ferguson *decision, which ruled that segregation was constitutional.*

after the Civil War and well into the 20th century. Lynching was used as a means of controlling and terrorizing African Americans to prevent them from voting or holding public office and to deprive them of their rights. Frequently, the victims were accused, often falsely, of a crime against a white person, and even a crime as minor as being disrespectful to or whistling at a white woman could result in lynching. Lisa Delpit, an African American educator and author, explained the implications of this widespread violence: "If ever, heaven forbid, an actual or imagined crime was

Marchers are shown here parading to the White House to give a petition to the president asking for justice in a lynching case.

committed by a black person against a white person, then the well-being of all black people was at risk, often serious physical risk."[12]

The preferred method of lynching was to hang victims. The white perpetrators of lynching were seldom prosecuted, and many lynchings were attended by prominent citizens, such as the mayor of a town.

A 2015 report by the Equal Justice Initiative (EJI) found that 4,384 African Americans were lynched as a result of racial terror from 1877 to 1950. However, lynching has occurred more recently, too. In 1998, three white men in Texas brutally murdered an African American man named James Byrd in a racially motivated attack. Although lynching is no longer common, racially motivated violence against black Americans continues to occur in different forms.

Continuing Effects After Desegregation

Segregation remained legal in the United States until 1954, when the Supreme Court overturned its earlier decision in *Plessy v. Ferguson*. The landmark case *Brown v. Board of Education* declared that separate schools for black and white students were unequal by their very nature and therefore unconstitutional. Throughout the remainder of the 1950s and into the 1960s, as schools and other public facilities were ordered to desegregate, the civil rights movement tried to end Jim Crow practices and ensure that African Americans had equal rights.

Although African Americans today are legally protected from segregation and discrimination, the effects of their long deprivation in the United States still remain. Asante, who calls for reparations in his book *Erasing Racism*, said, "The fact is, we cannot dispense with 250 years of involuntary servitude and sweep it under the rug. We cannot dispense with nearly one hundred years of official segregation."[13] Asante described the continuing effects of slavery on life for African Americans in the United States today:

> *Justice, for the descendants of the millions of Africans enslaved during that terrible period of American history, has eluded our society, and discussion of it creates unusually harsh reactions from many Americans. The lingering effects of the enslavement are current and immediate in almost all sectors of American life: health, education, employment, housing, and law.*[14]

A CHILD'S PERSPECTIVE

Lisa Delpit, an African American educator and author, recalled watching the popular TV show *Romper Room* and described how she became aware of racial discrimination as a child in the 1950s:

> *I learned early that Miss Pat, of* Romper Room*—no matter how much I looked into her magic mirror and no matter how good a "Do-Bee" I was—would not let me join her television classroom. "That's only for white kids," my mother explained. Things weren't as they seemed on television. She had to explain the connectedness of things initially beyond the grasp of my four-year-old, home-centered mind: somehow my "nappy" hair and my family's brown skin (I had yet to understand that my own "lighter" skin was irrelevant as long as it was embedded within a brown family) was connected to the workings of the larger world in ways that prevented me from sitting in Miss Pat's circle or from going to the bathroom while shopping downtown—and prevented my mother from trying on hats in a department store or from getting a teaching job closer to our house.*[1]

1. Lisa Delpit, *Other People's Children: Cultural Conflict in the Classroom*. New York, NY: New Press, 1995, p. 92.

Although it began its run with an all-white cast, the television show Romper Room *later had children of all races on the show and featured its first African American hostess, Miss Sharon Jeffery, in 1987.*

When Rosa Parks was arrested for refusing to give up her bus seat to a white man, her actions sparked the Montgomery bus boycott.

Randall Robinson, a civil rights activist and the author of *The Debt: What America Owes to Blacks*, explains sentiments that are shared by many African Americans about their history:

> *No race, no ethnic or religious group, has suffered so much over so long a span as blacks have, and do still, at the hands of those who benefited, with the connivance of the United States government, from slavery and the century of legalized American racial hostility that followed it.*[15]

Because the U.S. government has made reparations and apologized to other groups of people and their descendants, it seems reasonable to many people that reparations should also be made to African American descendants of slaves.

CHAPTER TWO
FIRST ATTEMPTS AT REPARATIONS

Former slaves and their descendants have sought reparations from the United States government since the end of the Civil War. Both groups believed their suffering and losses justified action from states, companies, and the federal government. Early attempts at reparations took different approaches, but none succeeded. Despite their failed attempts, these individuals pioneered the movement for slavery reparations in America.

The Freedmen's Bureau

The first attempt to provide some form of restitution to former slaves came in January 1865, a few months before the end of the Civil War. General William T. Sherman, whose famous march to the sea left a wide band of the Confederacy in ruins, met with 20 black community leaders in Savannah, Georgia. Sherman then issued Special Field Order No. 15, which outlined plans to distribute lands that had been confiscated from slaveholders in South Carolina, Georgia, and Florida to former slaves. This order was based on the conversations he had in Georgia and his observations of the destitute conditions former slaves were living in. The field order stated that each former slave family would receive a 40-acre (16 ha) plot of land and that "the islands from Charleston, south, the abandoned rice fields along the rivers for 30 miles back from the sea, and the country bordering the St. Johns River, Florida, are reserved and set apart for the settlement of the negroes now made free by the acts of war and the proclamation of the President of the United States."[16] Although mules were not mentioned in Sherman's order, it was widely believed that they had been promised so the freedmen had a way to till their land. Thus, the phrase "40 acres and a mule" represented the promise made by the U.S. government

The William Tecumseh Sherman Monument was erected in New York City in 1903 to honor General Sherman's leadership during the Civil War.

to help the freed slaves start new lives.

In March 1865, Congress established the Bureau of Refugees, Freedmen, and Abandoned Lands, commonly known as the Freedmen's Bureau, in part to help fulfill Sherman's order. The bureau was directed "to lease not more than forty acres of land within the Confederate states to each freedman or refugee for a period of three years; during or after the lease period, each occupant would be given the option to purchase the land for its value."[17] The bureau was in charge of a total of 800,000 acres (325,000 ha) of land that had been abandoned by or confiscated from Confederate landowners. Within 3 months of the establishment of the Freedmen's Bureau, 40,000 former slaves had relocated and begun to farm 400,000 acres (162,000 ha) of land they had been awarded in South Carolina and Georgia.

The land was, however, soon taken back from them. Not long after President Abraham Lincoln was

HELPING OUT FREEDMEN

The Bureau of Refugees, Freedmen, and Abandoned Lands—more commonly known as the Freedmen's Bureau—is one example of government efforts during Reconstruction to help former slaves overcome the disadvantages of enslavement. Established by Congress in March 1865, the bureau's main purpose was to provide food, medical supplies, and legal assistance to newly freed slaves after the Civil War. The Freedmen's Bureau also established schools to educate illiterate former slaves.

Another of the bureau's responsibilities was distributing land that had been abandoned by or confiscated from Southern landowners. These lands were supposed to be distributed in 40-acre (16 ha) lots to former slaves and those who could prove they remained loyal to the Union during the war. However, most of this land was instead returned to its original owners. The Freedmen's Bureau was disbanded in 1869, although its educational efforts continued until 1872. Its most important accomplishment was in education for former slaves. It spent $5 million to establish free public schools and higher education for black students in the South, including Howard, Fisk, and Atlanta universities and the Hampton Institute. By 1870, there were more than 1,000 schools in the South for freedmen.

In this map, green areas represent Union states, yellow areas represent Union states that permitted slavery, and red states represent the Confederacy.

President Andrew Johnson continually denied or removed any legislation that would have made reparations for slavery.

assassinated, his successor, President Andrew Johnson, revoked the policies set forth by Sherman's order and the Freedmen's Bureau. Johnson granted a pardon to former rebels and returned their lands to them. This was the same land that former slaves had been promised and had begun to farm. According to Congressman John Conyers Jr., "Land that had been distributed to Freedmen was reclaimed by the federal government and routed to the enslavers (who had lost the Civil War, fought for the Confederacy, and had already benefited unjustly from the unpaid labor of Africans)."[18] Only about 1,500 of these former slaves were able to keep their land. Author and historian Mary Frances Berry described the effect Johnson's actions had:

> *The government dashed the sea island freedmen's hopes after their hard work tilling land they thought was theirs. General Oliver Howard ... was ordered to either persuade or force blacks occupying the land under Sherman's orders to abandon their claims to their former owners and return to work for them as laborers. Incredulous, the freedmen cried out at the betrayal.*[19]

Due to the government's broken promise, the phrase "40 acres and a mule" came to represent the failure of the U.S. government to provide compensation or adequate assistance to the newly freed slaves. The phrase is still used today in discussing the post-Civil War treatment of black Americans and the fact that reparations for slavery have not been made. Berry pointed out that "freedom for ... ex-slaves would have been very different if the Union had kept its promises to give them land confiscated from Confederate slaveholders. The reparations question could have been settled at once."[20]

Land for Former Slaves

A year after Sherman's unfulfilled promise, Congress enacted the Southern Homestead Act (1866). Under this act, the head of a family received 80 acres (32 ha) of land and was allowed six months to purchase the property at the low rate of only $5. This act applied to people of all races, not just former slaves, and was intended to encourage people to settle outside of heavily populated Southern towns.

Approximately 1,000 black individuals received land under the act, which was far fewer than would have received land under Sherman's Special Field Order No. 15. The land distributed under this act was generally of poor quality or was located in remote areas.

In some cases, it was already claimed by lumber companies. Additionally, most former slaves were desperately poor and therefore, could not afford to purchase land, even at the special low rate. They also could not afford to feed and support themselves for months while they waited for their crops to grow. Scholars Ronald P. Salzberger and Mary C. Turck explained the outcome of the Southern Homestead Act for the freed slaves: "Whether by foreclosure or by terrorist threats, most black families lost the land they had purchased. Without land, they were once again reduced to dependence on white landowners and employers."[21]

The situation was not helped by President Andrew Johnson, who vetoed any proposal to provide land to freed slaves. Among the proposals he refused to sign was one to colonize African Americans in the West, along the Union Pacific Railroad. There, they could have land as well as provide labor and protection to the railroad. Another proposal was to provide African American soldiers stationed in Texas with homesteads there and enough rations to survive until their crops grew. Again, Johnson vetoed this plan. According to one researcher, "President Johnson seemed to be determined to make sure that freedmen received no land. He mercilessly vetoed any proposal having to do with providing land to the freedmen that reached his desk."[22]

Legislative Attempts at Reparations

In 1867, Congressman Thaddeus Stevens, who had been an outspoken opponent of slavery and was instrumental in the passage of the 14th Amendment, introduced a bill to Congress called the African Slave Reparations Bill (H.R. 20). It proposed to have public lands in all 10 former Confederate states turned over to the federal government. Former slaves would receive 40 acres (16 ha) of this land along with $50 per homestead. Under pressure from Southern lawmakers, Johnson vetoed the bill. However, the idea of seeking monetary compensation for former slaves did not end there.

The next attempt to aid former slaves was a bill seeking government pensions for African Americans. Black soldiers had fought in the Union army, and they and their families, including their widows and children, were entitled to the same veterans' pensions provided to white veterans. Many black veterans had trouble obtaining these pensions because they did not have the proper paperwork, such as birth certificates and marriage licenses.

CONGRESSMAN STEVENS'S BILL

In 1867, Congressman Thaddeus Stevens, a longtime abolitionist, introduced the African Slave Reparations Bill to Congress. He spoke before the U.S. House of Representatives of the necessity of such a bill for former slaves and their descendants. The following is an excerpt from his speech:

> *Four million persons have just been freed from a condition of dependence, wholly unacquainted with business transactions, kept systematically in ignorance of all their rights and of the common elements of education, without which none of any race are competent to earn an honest living ... Make them independent of their old masters, so that they may not be compelled to work for them upon unfair terms, which can only be done by giving them a small tract of land to cultivate for themselves ... Nothing is so likely to make a man a good citizen as to make him a freeholder ... Nothing will make men so industrious and moral as to let them feel that they are above want and are the owners of the soil which they till.*[1]

1. Quoted in Direct Black Action, "Thaddeus Stevens Speaks to Congress About Reparations for the African Slaves and Their Descendants." www.directblackaction.com/rep_bills/stevens_hr29.txt.

Along with his 14th Amendment work, Congressman Thaddeus Stevens was also instrumental in passing legislation for a free public school system in Pennsylvania.

Partly for this reason, in 1890, Walter R. Vaughan, a white Democrat and a former editor of the Omaha, Nebraska, *Daily Democrat*, proposed a pension for former slaves that was modeled after the Union veterans' pension. He persuaded William J. Connell, his Nebraska congressman, to introduce the Ex-slave Pension and Bounty Bill in 1890. The bill considered any black person born before 1861 to have been a slave and therefore eligible for the proposed pension, unless other documentation was provided to prove otherwise.

The plan also called for one-time payments as well as monthly benefits that were based on the person's age and would increase in time. For example, former slaves who were more than 70 years of age would receive a one-time payment (called a bounty) of $500 and a monthly pension of $15. Former slaves who were between 60 and 69 years of age would receive a bounty of $300 and a monthly pension of $12.

Vaughan's interest in seeking pensions for former slaves was only partly motivated by a concern for the well-being of the freedmen and freedwomen in the South. Although he was disturbed at the state of poverty he witnessed among former slaves during a trip he took through Mississippi in 1870, he was also eager to help the economy of the South. Vaughan reasoned that if the former slaves received pensions, they would have more money to spend and thereby help revive the Southern economy, which had been devastated by the Civil War. The bill was not, however, supported by the three black members of Congress, who instead advocated voting rights and federal aid for education as the way for black Americans to escape from poverty. Ultimately, Congress rejected the pension bill, although other similar bills were proposed in the late 1890s.

In 1898, Congressman Jeremiah Botkin introduced a bill that would give former slaves 40-acre (16 ha) homesteads, or 160 acres (64.75 ha) for a family. This bill, which was reminscent of Sherman's original promise, did not pass. A Senate bill to appropriate $100,000 to create a home in Washington, D.C., for elderly former slaves was sponsored by Senator George Perkins in 1895. One congressman said of this bill, "There is no question that the aged and colored people who once were slaves are more subject to destitution and require charitable aid more than any other class of people in the United States."[23] However, many black activists of the time were opposed to this bill because the size of the proposed facility was too small to accommodate all the eligible former slaves. They also thought that if this bill passed, it would end the question of any other form of reparations.

Vaughan abandoned the pursuit of pensions for former slaves when the U.S. Post Office and the Pension Bureau investigated him for fraud, but the bill he had helped introduce would have a far-reaching effect for former slaves.

Callie House and the Ex-Slave Association

In 1891, Vaughan wrote a pamphlet titled *Freedmen's Pension Bill: A Plea for American Freedmen* that sold 10,000 copies at $1 apiece. This pamphlet caught the attention of several former slaves who in 1896 founded their own organization, the National Ex-Slave Mutual Relief, Bounty, and Pension Association, in Nashville, Tennessee. Two years later, a laundress named Callie House, who was born into slavery, was elected the assistant secretary of the association. House became the driving force behind the organization and was considered to be its leader.

The purpose of the Ex-Slave Association was twofold. The first was lobbying to pass the pension bill. House traveled extensively throughout the South collecting petitions that included former slaves' names, ages, and former masters. Thousands of African Americans signed these petitions, urging Congress to compensate them for their forced labor during slavery. The second purpose of the association was providing mutual assistance to its members, each of whom paid monthly dues of 10 cents.

By the early 20th century, the association had about 300,000 members. House stated, "If the Government had the right to free us she had a right to make some provision for us and since she did not make it soon after Emancipation she ought to make it now."[24] Famed abolitionist Frederick Douglass supported the reparations movement, and said in a letter to Vaughan, "The Egyptian bondsmen went out with the spoils of his master, and the Russian serf was provided with farming tools and three acres of land with which to begin life,—but the Negro has neither spoils, implements nor lands, and today, he is practically a slave on the very plantation where formerly he was driven to toil under the lash."[25]

In 1915, House hired a well-known African American lawyer named Cornelius Jones to represent the Ex-Slave Association in a class action lawsuit against the U.S. Department of the Treasury. Jones calculated the value of the former slaves' labor to be

Callie House, a former slave, was the unofficial leader of the Ex-Slave Association and sued the government for monetary reparations.

A LETTER FROM CALLIE HOUSE

The following letter was sent by Callie House to the membership of the National Ex-Slave Mutual Relief, Bounty, and Pension Association after she was elected assistant secretary in 1898. The letter appeals to all organizations seeking the enactment of the Ex-slave Pension and Bounty Bill, also known as the Mason Bill, to work together in seeking compensation for former slaves:

It is my firm belief that honest labor should be rewarded, regardless of the color of the man or woman who performs that labor. I am in favor of the principles embodied in the so-called Mason Bill because they are just, and should the Bill receive the consideration it richly merits, it will, in my opinion, be but a question of time when those of our race who have borne the burden and heat of the day, will receive some recompense for honest labor performed during the dark and bitter days of slavery.

Let us consolidate all ex-slave organizations and bring to bear upon the law makers of the country which we labored so long and well to develop, every degree of influence within our power.

Very truly,
Callie House[1]

1. Quoted in Mary Frances Berry, *My Face Is Black Is True: Callie House and the Struggle for Ex-Slave Reparations*. New York, NY: Knopf, 2005, p. 78.

$68 million. The money, Jones and House suggested, would come from the cotton tax—a federal tax on confiscated raw cotton that was first enacted in 1862 to help pay war debts. The money was still in a fund in the U.S. Treasury, and because the federal government had profited from the sale of cotton produced through unpaid slave labor, Jones argued in federal court that the money should be paid to the former slaves. The court rejected their claim. Secretary of the Treasury William McAdoo stated that the tax had been unconstitutional in the first place, and furthermore, "the money collected as a

Civil War revenue tax has been treated as part of the general receipts of the Government and applied to payment of government debts ... There is no fund of $68,000,000 or any other sum in the Treasury of the United States for ex-slaves, or those who worked in the cotton fields of the South."[26]

Jones appealed the case to the U.S. Supreme Court, which upheld the earlier decision.

An End to the Pension Movement

In addition to losing the lawsuit against the treasury, House and Jones faced other legal problems in their efforts to seek pensions for former slaves. Alarmed by the rapidly swelling membership of the Ex-Slave Association, as well as by the lawsuit, the federal government targeted the leaders of the association in an effort to stop their activities. According to Berry, "The government charged Jones with fraud for mailing letters seeking support from African Americans who might benefit from the lawsuit. The government sought to punish Jones for having the temerity [confidence] to bring the lawsuit and for his connection to the Ex-Slave Association."[27]

Although the government ultimately decided against prosecuting Jones for fraud, they did bring charges of fraud against House and other leaders of the pension movement in 1916. According to one writer, House was charged with "acting fraudulently by collecting money to fund a lobbying effort that instilled the false hope in the hearts of the ex-slaves that the government would give them a pension."[28] The government's reasoning was that House and other movement leaders were defrauding and exploiting people by taking their money to fight for legislation that would never be passed. Furthermore, the government charged that House had used the Ex-Slave Association for her own personal expenses.

Although there was no proof that she had misused any association funds, House was convicted and imprisoned for one year in the Missouri state prison. Her conviction and imprisonment led to the demise of the Ex-Slave Association's efforts to seek pensions, although the association continued to provide mutual assistance to its members. House died in 1928, and with her passing, the association disbanded. However, interest in the movement she had helped to found continued.

Possible Return to Africa

Some of the former agents of the National Ex-Slave Mutual Relief, Bounty, and Pension Association turned to a new leader—Marcus Garvey. Garvey, who was born in Jamaica, had traveled extensively in South America, Central America, and England before moving to the United States in 1916. He founded the Universal Negro Improvement Association (UNIA) in 1914, and he established several branches in the United States. They ultimately attracted 2 million members worldwide. His organization, which supported civil rights, self-help, racial pride, and reparations for slavery, attracted many of the Ex-Slave Association's former members.

Garvey and the UNIA saw repatriation, or returning, to Africa as the solution to the question of reparations for slavery. This idea was not new; the American Colonization Society had helped send thousands of freed American slaves to the African nation of Liberia in the early 1800s. Garvey founded the Black Star Steamship Line in 1919 to transport former slaves and their descendants to Africa. He sought to establish a black-governed country in Africa and petitioned the League of Nations after World War I for the former German colonies there. Like many others before him, Garvey was unsuccessful in his fight for reparations.

In 1922, the U.S. government brought the same charges of mail fraud against Garvey that it had brought against House. Garvey was convicted and spent two years in prison; upon his release, he was deported to Jamaica. Garvey's conviction, imprisonment, and deportation brought about the end of the Black Star Steamship Line and the UNIA. However, many former members of the UNIA became advocates in the struggle for reparations, and Garvey's work continued to influence black leaders in the 20th century, including activist Malcolm X.

Moore and the Reparations Committee

Despite the demise of the Ex-Slave Association and the UNIA in the late 1920s, some aging former slaves continued to ask the government about pensions. In 1928, the relatives of a former slave asked U.S. Attorney General John Sargent, "Is there any money set aside for old ex-slaves by the U.S. Government?"[29] Similar queries were sent to Presidents Herbert Hoover and Franklin D. Roosevelt in the 1930s. One former slave asked Roosevelt what had happened to the idea of "giving us pensions in payment for our long days of servitude?"[30]

One former member of the UNIA who continued the call for slave reparations was Audley Moore. Born in 1898, Moore was the descendant of former slaves; her grandmother had been

REPATRIATION TO AFRICA

Early efforts to compensate freed slaves included the movement to send them back to Africa. In 1822, 86 former slaves were transported from the United States to Liberia with the help of the American Colonization Society. Another 19,000 followed over the next 40 years. After the Civil War, there was renewed interest in resettling freed black individuals in Africa. However, African Americans sensed that white Americans wanted to get rid of the newly freed slaves by deporting them. Many African Americans also regarded the United States as their home and wanted to stay. Richard H. Cain, an African American congressman from South Carolina during the 1870s, spoke against the idea of repatriation:

> *You have brought us here, and here we are going to stay. We are not going one foot or one inch from this land. Our mothers and fathers and our grandfathers and great-grandfathers have died here. Here we have sweated. Here we have toiled. Here we have made this country great and rich by our labor and toil. It is mean in you now to want to drive us away, after having taken all of our toil for 200 years.*[1]

1. Quoted in John David Smith, *Black Voices from Reconstruction, 1865–1877*. Gainesville, FL: University of Florida Press, 1997, p. 146.

the daughter of a slaveholder. Moore had a lifelong commitment to the civil rights movement, and she organized the first organization during World War I to provide medical and other care to African American soldiers who were denied care for racial reasons. In 1955, Moore founded the Reparations Committee of Descendants of United States Slaves, and in 1962, the committee filed a reparations claim in California.

In addition, Moore petitioned the United Nations (UN) in 1962 to demand that the United States be required to pay reparations for slavery. On the 100th anniversary of the Emancipation Proclamation in 1863, Moore presented President John F. Kennedy with a petition containing more than 1 million signatures that demanded reparations from the government. Although none of Moore's efforts were successful during her lifetime, she continued as an active spokesperson for the reparations movement until her death in 1997.

The initial efforts to provide help and care for former slaves, including Reconstruction's "40 acres and a mule," the congressional bills, and the pension movements, all failed to gain satisfactory recompense for the effects of slavery. Although ultimately unsuccessful, the work of former slaves and slave descendants, including House, Garvey, and Moore, laid the groundwork for the civil rights activists of the mid-20th century.

CHAPTER THREE
REPARATIONS FROM THE 1960s TO TODAY

Heading into the 1960s, the reparations movement grew increasingly complicated. The majority of former slaves were deceased, so the movement now sought reparations for descendants of former slaves. De facto (in practice) and de jure (by law) discrimination also continued to worsen in America, and African Americans faced discrimination on a daily basis. The reparations movement now sought to include compensation for enduring discrimination that resulted from slavery.

Following the Civil War, the integration of freed blacks into society was a complex and controversial social and political issue, and racial segregation perpetuated the sentiments of white superiority and black inferiority that existed during slavery.

Prominent black political activists, including Martin Luther King Jr. and Malcolm X, gave their lives for the civil rights movement and the advancement of black people. Many other black leaders pushed forward and demanded reparations in the form of cash payments or social programs. To date, some progress has been made. However, the battle for slavery reparations is far from over, as no large-scale government reparations program has been put in place.

The Civil Rights Movement

The 1960s was a decade of great social upheaval in the United States, beginning with the civil rights movement. Civil rights leaders worked hard to guarantee the basic rights of citizenship for African Americans. One important piece of legislation was the Civil Rights Act of 1964, which banned discrimination in employment and public accommodations. Schools and universities began to desegregate, along with other public facilities, including libraries and courthouses. Privately owned

The Martin Luther King Jr. Memorial in Washington, D.C., was built to honor King's legacy and leadership in the civil rights movement.

establishments, such as restaurants, hotels, and theaters, soon followed.

By the middle of the decade, calls for reparations for slavery had been incorporated into the civil rights movement. One example of a public appeal for reparations came from King in his 1964 book *Why We Can't Wait*. King wrote,

> *No amount of gold could provide an adequate compensation for the exploitation and humiliation of the Negro in America down through the centuries ... Yet a price can be placed on unpaid wages. The ancient common law has always provided a remedy for the appropriation of the labor of*

DEVASTATING RACE RIOTS

In the 1920s, two devastating race riots took place in the United States. The first occurred in Tulsa, Oklahoma, in 1921. The riot was sparked by false accusations of a black man raping a white woman. As many as 300 people were killed by a white mob, and the majority of the predominantly African American Greenwood district was demolished.

In 2000, a report commissioned by the state of Oklahoma recommended that $12 million in reparations be paid to the families of the victims. However, the state refused to pay. The governor said, "A state law prohibits Oklahoma from making reparations for any past mass crime committed by its officials or on the state's behalf."[1]

A race riot that occurred in Rosewood, Florida, in 1923 was also sparked by the false claim by a white woman that she was raped by a black man. A white mob completely destroyed an all-black neighborhood, burning houses to the ground and killing six black residents. The violence destroyed the homes of 25 to 30 families who lived there, and the community was never rebuilt. In 1994, Florida passed the Rosewood Compensation Act, which paid each of the nine survivors $150,000 and created a scholarship fund.

1. Quoted in Hongyu Wang and Nadine Olson, eds., *A Journey to Unlearn and Learn in Multicultural Education*. New York, NY: Peter Lang, 2009, p. 66.

In 1921, a race riot broke out in Tulsa, Oklahoma. During the riot, churches were set on fire, people were killed, and an entire African American neighborhood was destroyed.

one human being by another. This law should be made to apply for American Negroes. The payment should be in the form of a massive program by the government of special, compensatory measures which could be regarded as a settlement in accordance with the accepted practice of common law.[31]

Another prominent civil rights activist, Malcolm X, also supported reparations for slavery. In 1964, after traveling and speaking in Africa, Malcolm gave a speech in Paris in which he explained his belief that reparations for slavery is still a valid issue a full century after slavery's abolishment in the United States:

The only reason that the present generation of white Americans are in a position of economic strength ... is because their fathers worked our fathers for over 400 years with no pay ... We were sold from plantation to plantation like you sell a horse, or a cow, or a chicken, or a bushel of wheat ... All that money ... is what gives the present generation of American whites the ability to walk around the earth with their

Malcolm X was assassinated in 1965 as he was taking the stage to address the Organization of Afro-American Unity in New York City.

> *chest out ... like they have some kind of economic ingenuity.*[32]

Equal Employment Opportunities

The Civil Rights Act of 1964 also established the Equal Employment Opportunity Commission, leading the way to the U.S. policy of affirmative action. Affirmative action was implemented to ensure that all job applicants and employees would be treated fairly, regardless of their race, religion, gender, or national origin. It also mandated that specific underserved groups, including women and black applicants, were to be given preferential treatment in hiring practices and university admissions to make up for past discrimination against them. In this way, affirmative action can be seen as a form of reparations for slavery and racial discrimination.

Prominent people, such as Martin Luther King Jr. and Presidents John F. Kennedy and Lyndon B. Johnson, saw reparations as a necessary and proactive method to compensate for the effects of decades of discriminatory hiring practices.

Many Americans view Johnson as a champion of civil rights. At his funeral in 1973, one black woman stood before his casket and told her daughter, "People don't know it, but he did more for us than anybody, any president, ever did."[33] Johnson firmly believed in the policy of affirmative action. During a June 4, 1965, commencement address he delivered at Howard University (a predominantly African American school in Washington, D.C.), Johnson spoke of the problems African Americans faced as a result of slavery and segregation and explained why he believed affirmative action was fair:

> *You do not wipe away the scars of centuries by saying: Now you are free to go where you want, and do as you desire, and choose the leaders you please.*
>
> *You do not take a person who, for years, has been hobbled by chains and liberate him, bring him up to the starting line of a race and then say, "you are free to compete with all the others," and still justly believe that you have been completely fair ...*
>
> *Perhaps most important—its influence radiating to every part of life—is the breakdown of the Negro family structure.*

For this, most of all, white America must accept responsibility. It flows from centuries of oppression and persecution of the Negro man. It flows from the long years of degradation and discrimination, which have attacked his dignity and assaulted his ability to produce for his family.[34]

Johnson took concrete action to ease the effects of slavery and discrimination, including his War on Poverty, Great Society, and affirmative action programs. These programs, however, were abandoned by later administrations. Beginning in the mid-1990s, states including California, Washington, Texas, Louisiana, Mississippi, and Florida banned affirmative action in college admissions. Thus, the earlier gains of affirmative action were reversed, and the perception many people have of unaddressed wrongs has continued.

James Forman's Demands for Reparation

During the rapid political and social change in the late 1960s, James Forman rose to the forefront of the reparations movement. Forman was an African American civil rights leader and former executive director of the Student Nonviolent Coordinating Committee (SNCC), which was dedicated to ending segregation in the South. In 1969, Forman and his supporters marched into the all-white Riverside Church in New York City, interrupting Sunday service. Forman stood at the pulpit and read aloud his "Black Manifesto," which was an appeal for reparations. The introduction to the manifesto begins with the words: "Brothers and Sisters: We have come from all over the country, burning with anger and despair not only with the miserable economic plight of our people, but fully aware that the racism on which the Western World was built dominates our lives."[35] The manifesto continued:

We the black people ... are fully aware that we have been forced to come together because racist white America has exploited our resources, our minds, our bodies, our labor. For centuries we have been forced to live as colonized people inside the United States, victimized by the most vicious, racist system in the world. We have helped to build the most industrial country in the world.[36]

Whereas previous civil rights leaders such as Malcolm X and King had called for reparations in broad terms, Forman's appeal was specific. In the

"NEGRO POVERTY IS NOT WHITE POVERTY"

In the June 4, 1965, commencement address at Howard University in Washington, D.C., President Lyndon B. Johnson spoke of the great disparities between black and white Americans in terms of employment, income, poverty, and infant mortality rates. He said there were two main causes for the differences: The first was poverty, and the second was "the devastating heritage of long years of slavery; and a century of oppression, hatred, and injustice." Johnson continued,

> *For Negro poverty is not white poverty. Many of its causes and many of its cures are the same. But there are differences—deep, corrosive, obstinate differences—radiating painful roots into the community, and into the family, and the nature of the individual.*
>
> *These differences are not racial differences. They are solely and simply the consequence of ancient brutality, past injustice, and present prejudice. They are anguishing to observe. For the Negro, they are a constant reminder of oppression. For the white, they are a constant reminder*

"Black Manifesto," he demanded $500 million in reparations from churches and synagogues for the segregation and exploitation of black Americans. Forman said this amount came to $15 for each black person in the United States. The manifesto outlined in detail how the funds were to be used, including banks, publishing and printing, television networks, a research center to study the problems of black people, a training center for black people to gain a variety of communication skills, a better welfare system, and a black university in the South. All of these things, according to Forman, were "only a beginning of the reparations due us as a people who have been exploited and degraded, brutalized, killed, and persecuted."[37]

Many people thought Forman's demands were unrealistic and excessive. An editorial in the *New York Times* stated, "There is neither wealth

of guilt. But they must be faced and they must be dealt with and they must be overcome, if we are ever to reach the time when the only difference between Negroes and whites is the color of their skin.[1]

1. Quoted in "President Lyndon B. Johnson's Commencement Address at Howard University: 'To Fulfill These Rights,'" Lyndon Baines Johnson Library and Museum. www.lbjlib.utexas.edu/johnson/archives.hom/speeches.hom/650604.asp.

Lyndon B. Johnson, the president of the United States from 1963 to 1969, signed the landmark Civil Rights Act of 1964.

nor wisdom enough in the world to compensate in money for all the wrongs in history."[38] Black civil rights activist Bayard Rustin also criticized the "Black Manifesto," saying, "The idea of reparations is a ridiculous idea. If my great-grandfather picked cotton for 50 years, then he may deserve some money, but he's dead and gone and nobody owes me anything."[39]

Despite these criticisms, others supported the idea of reparations for slavery. In response to the "Black Manifesto," the religious journal *Christian Century* wrote, "We do not believe the idea of reparations is ridiculous. This generation of blacks continues to pay the price of earlier generations' slavery and subjugation; this generation of whites continues to enjoy the profits of racial exploitation."[40]

The "Black Manifesto" sparked controversy. However, the controversy soon faded away, and Forman's

Unlike other civil rights leaders, activist James Forman demanded very specific reparations in his "Black Manifesto."

demands for monetary compensation were not met. It would be two decades before another official proposal surrounding the issue of reparations was made—this time, not from the pulpit of a church but from the floor of Congress.

Reparation Legislation

In 1989, Representative John Conyers Jr. of Michigan proposed a bill titled H.R. 40, the Commission to Study Reparation Proposals for African Americans Act. The bill proposes a seven-member commission to study the issue of reparations for U.S. slavery.

Conyers was inspired to introduce the bill by the Civil Liberties Act of 1988, with which Congress apologized to Japanese Americans who had been detained in internment camps during World War II and paid them damages of $20,000 each. Conyers named his bill H.R. 40 because the number 40 holds a special significance for African Americans. Conyers explained, "I chose the number of the bill, 40, as a symbol of the forty acres and a mule that the United States initially promised freed slaves. This unfulfilled promise and the serious devastation that slavery had on African American lives has never been officially recognized by the United States Government."[41] H.R. 40 sought a formal apology for slavery in addition to a commission to study slavery's effect on African Americans. The end goal of the bill was to determine whether compensation was due to the descendants of former slaves. The opening paragraph of the bill states its purpose:

> *To acknowledge the fundamental injustice, cruelty, brutality, and inhumanity of slavery in the United States and the 13 American colonies between 1619 and 1865 and to establish a commission to examine the institution of slavery, subsequent de jure [according to law] and de facto [in reality] racial and economic discrimination against African Americans, and the impact of these forces on living African Americans, to make recommendations to the Congress on appropriate remedies, and for other purposes.*[42]

The bill did not make a proposal for specific reparations but merely asked for a commission to study the issue and make a recommendation on the matter. Although Conyers first introduced the bill in Congress in 1989 and has reintroduced it every year since, the bill has yet to make it out of committee. This means that the House of Representatives has not yet been allowed to vote on whether or

BLACK TAX CLAIMS SCAM

During the 1990s and early 2000s, many African Americans fraudulently filed so-called "black tax" claims with the Internal Revenue Service (IRS). They did this by reporting a tax credit for slavery reparations on their tax returns. Many of the claims were in the amount of $43,209 each, which was the estimated current value of 40 acres and a mule. In 2001, 80,000 such claims were filed, many of them by dishonest accountants who charged $700 to file the claims.

Several of these claims were actually paid in error by the IRS. Calling it the biggest tax scam they had ever seen, the IRS brought lawsuits against people who had prepared returns claiming the "black tax." Anyone who received a refund in error had to pay it back with accrued interest. Those who had already spent the money had to work out a repayment schedule with the IRS. In addition, some people have been fined $500 for filing frivolous tax returns. Although it was an illegal attempt at gaining reparations for slavery, it did bring attention to the issue and further promote the cause.

not to send it to the Senate for further review. However, the bill has continued to gain support and was most recently reintroduced in the updated legislation for the 115th Congress in January 2017.

In 1997, Representative Tony Hall of Ohio introduced a similar piece of legislation calling on the U.S. government to issue a formal apology for slavery. The bill was not adopted, but it prompted Hall to introduce the Apology for Slavery Resolution in 2000. Hall's second piece of proposed legislation did not make it out of committee. Hall wrote of the necessity for an official apology for slavery from the U.S. government:

> *Unfortunately, America's history is littered with many examples of missed opportunities to address the "peculiar institution" of slavery. When our Founding Fathers declared that "all men are created equal," we could have truly included everyone. When we established the Constitution as the rule of law for our new country, we could have treated slaves as full and equal, instead of treating them as three-fifths of a person.*

> *When the Supreme Court made its rulings, when our nation amended the Constitution, or when Congress wrote Civil Rights laws—at any of these moments in our history, we could have apologized for slavery. But we failed, and now we must go back and finish our history's chapter on slavery.*[43]

Like Hall's previous bill and the one introduced by Conyers, this piece of legislation seeks an official government acknowledgement and an apology for slavery. One criticism of the bill is that it does not call for specific monetary compensation. Proponents of the reparations movement feel that neither bill is worded strongly enough.

Numerous other proposals at the state and city levels have experienced various levels of success, including a reparations bill very similar to H.R. 40 introduced in Michigan by State Representative Ed Vaughn. Also in Michigan, State Representative Derrick Hale introduced a bill that would allow tax credits for African Americans. These two Michigan bills have been met with general opposition. California passed the Slavery Era Disclosure Law in 2000 that requires insurance companies to disclose their records on African Americans who were held as slaves. Illinois, Iowa, and Maryland all followed suit in 2003, 2004, and 2009, respectively.

Similarly, cities including Philadelphia, Pennsylvania; Chicago, Illinois; Milwaukee, Wisconsin; Oakland, California; San Francisco, California; Detroit, Michigan; Berkeley, California; and Richmond, Virginia, require companies doing business with the city to disclose their historical ties to slavery. New York City has adopted a resolution to study reparations for slave descendants. Additionally, California enacted a law requiring the University of California to research the economic legacy of slavery.

Farmer-Paellmann versus Corporate America

In addition to supporting such legislation, the reparations movement has gone to court. The most prominent and successful court case was brought by Deadria Farmer-Paellmann, a legal activist and the great-great-granddaughter of a slave. In 2002, she filed a class action lawsuit in federal court on behalf of 35 million African Americans. The lawsuit targeted the profits gained through slave labor by three companies: FleetBoston Financial, the insurance company Aetna, and the railroad firm CSX. Farmer-Paellmann explained,

Deadria Farmer-Paellmann runs the Restitution Study Group, which uses DNA testing to unite families that were separated because of slavery.

"These are corporations that benefited from stealing people, from stealing labor, from forced breeding, from torture, from committing numerous horrendous acts, and there's no reason why they should be able to hold onto assets they acquired through such horrendous acts."[44]

FleetBoston is the successor to Providence Bank, which the lawsuit states was founded by John Brown, a Rhode Island slave trader. Likewise, CSX is the successor of various railroads built and run in part with slave labor, according to the lawsuit. The third company, Aetna, issued slave life insurance policies to slaveholders, thereby benefiting from the slave trade. According to Farmer-Paellmann,

> *Slave life insurance policies were written with slave holders as the beneficiaries. An investor, unsure about purchasing costly human chattel, would gain security from predecessor companies to Aetna Inc., New York Life Insurance Company, even American International Group. The policies essentially meant: "go ahead and buy those Africans. If they die, we've got you covered. You can buy another one." Slave policies helped slave owners to employ enslaved Africans in ultra hazardous capacities. Consequently, insured enslaved Africans sometimes died horrendous deaths—for example, drowning or burning to death in coal mines.*[45]

After learning of Farmer-Paellmann's plan to sue them, Aetna apologized to African Americans in March 2000 for its role in supporting slavery. It also made reparations by establishing a scholarship fund and internship program for minorities.

Official Public Apologies

Apologizing to African Americans for slavery, as Aetna did, is viewed as a form of reparation. Public apologies, while mostly symbolic gestures, are seen as an important step toward reconciliation and healing past wounds.

Several public apologies have been issued in recent years, including one that was printed on the front page of the *Hartford Courant* in 2000. The Connecticut newspaper apologized for having run advertisements for slave auctions in the past. Other prominent groups and companies have apologized publicly for their role in slavery and racism, including the Southern Baptist Convention, JP Morgan Chase & Co., and Wachovia (now Wells Fargo).

In February 2007, Virginia became the first state to issue an official apology for its role in slavery. The fact that Virginia was where the first African Americans arrived in the New World made the apology especially significant. According to the official resolution,

> *[Government-sanctioned slavery] ranks as the most horrendous of all depredations of human rights and violations of our founding ideals in our nation's history, and the abolition of slavery was followed by systematic discrimination, enforced segregation, and other insidious institutions and practices toward Americans of African descent that were rooted in racism, racial bias, and racial misunderstanding.*[46]

The Southern Baptist Convention apologized for its role in slavery in 1995 and continues to advocate for nondiscrimination within its churches.

Maryland, North Carolina, Alabama, New Jersey, Florida, Tennessee, and Connecticut followed Virginia's lead and apologized from 2007 to 2009. Delaware also did so in 2016. In each apology, the state admitted its role, acknowledged the horrors of slavery, and sought forgiveness for its actions.

On June 18, 2009, the U.S. Senate apologized for the Jim Crow laws and the institution of slavery. Concurrent resolution 26 by the 111th Congress stated,

> *Whereas an apology for centuries of brutal dehumanization and injustices cannot erase the past, but confession of the wrongs committed and a formal apology to African Americans will help bind the wounds of the Nation that are rooted in slavery and can speed racial healing and reconciliation and help the people of the United States understand the past and honor the history of all people of the United States.*[47]

This resolution apologizes for slavery and segregation and expresses an intention to move the nation toward reconciliation and peaceful living.

The House passed a resolution in 2008, but a single resolution has yet to pass through both chambers and then earn approval from the sitting president. This means that the U.S. government as a whole has never officially apologized for its role in the slavery era. At times, the government did come close. Presidents Bill Clinton, George W. Bush, and Barack Obama each acknowledged that slavery was wrong, but no president has ever issued a formal apology.

Efforts to obtain reparations for slavery continue, however, and the reparations movement has gained supporters in recent years. While some successes in various forms have been achieved, no real reparations for slavery as such have been offered. One main reason for this is that slavery reparations still remain an extremely complicated and controversial issue in the United States.

CHAPTER FOUR
THE REALITY OF REPARATIONS

Slavery ended long enough ago that current U.S. citizens are neither former slaves nor former slaveholders. This makes the issue of reparations for slavery complicated. Finding a solution or programs that would please a majority requires answering many questions. What form should reparations take? Who should benefit? Who should pay? Some may even question if reparations are deserved at all. The answers to these questions vary depending on the scholar, citizen, civil rights group, government official, or company that is asked. The key to reparations will require reaching an agreement, or at least a compromise, on some of the answers to those questions. Only then can the movement move forward and find widespread success.

The Passage of Time

Slavery was officially abolished in the United States more than 150 years ago, and legalized segregation ended more than 50 years ago. The time between those events and today may complicate efforts to obtain reparations for slavery and its aftermath in several ways. Some people believe that the passage of time makes it increasingly difficult to trace people's ancestry and therefore determine their level or degree of victimization or guilt. Some also believe that the passage of so much time allows the introduction of new factors into the reparations equation, such as people who immigrated to the United States after slavery was abolished. Are recent white immigrants responsible for contributing to reparations? Are recent black immigrants entitled to receive reparations? The growing numbers of biracial or multiracial Americans creates additional complications to identifying those who may be responsible for contributing toward or eligible to receive reparations.

Some children have one white parent and one black parent, so they could be the descendants of both slaves and slaveholders.

There is also the question of the statute of limitations. Statutes of limitations are laws that regulate the amount of time a victim has to take legal action following a crime. If a crime is not prosecuted within this length of time, then the victim or victims lose the right to seek legal action for the crime. The length of statutes of limitations varies depending on the crime, with more serious crimes having a longer statute of limitations. Some crimes, such as murder, war crimes, and crimes against humanity, have no statute of limitations on them, meaning that charges can be brought no matter how long ago the crime occurred.

It is unclear whether seeking reparations for slavery has a statute of limitations or, if so, what the statute of limitations would be. Many people say there is no statute of limitations when it comes to slavery because it was a human rights abuse. As Robinson points out, "We are talking about crimes by governments against people, crimes that should not be touched by statutes of limitations, because when governments commit such crimes, they 'have a certain immortality.'"[48]

Law professor Jon M. van Dyke agrees that the statute of limitations should not apply to the enslavement of black Americans because it constituted a crime against humanity. He also believes that slavery should be exempt from any statute of limitations because of equitable tolling. Equitable tolling suspends time limits in cases where the victim or victims are prevented from seeking legal action at an earlier date. Van Dyke stated, "It certainly would have been unrealistic for African Americans to have brought a suit for reparations at any time prior to the present period, since they were subject to active, officially sanctioned discrimination until recently."[49] Furthermore, van Dyke asserts that "the duty to address violations of fundamental human rights continues as long as the consequences of those violations continue to scar a community."[50]

If there is no statute of limitations on human rights crimes, then how far back in history are people allowed to go in seeking reparations for past wrongs? Some people wonder whether allowing African Americans to sue for reparations and apologies for slavery would open the doors to other groups suing for past offenses. Writing about people who are critical of addressing past wrongs without a statute of limitation, Columbia Law School professor Suzette Malveaux wrote, "Opponents [of reparations] argue that reparations claims should be time-barred because their age complicates the identification of the parties, causation, and remedies; compromises deterrence; undermines repose; and does not warrant equitable treatment."[51]

There are, however, precedents for making restitution and apologies today for acts that occurred as long ago as the mid-19th century. For example, former U.K. Prime Minister Tony Blair apologized in 1997 to the Irish for the way the British government treated their ancestors during the Great Famine, which took place from 1845 to 1850. In the United States, the Sand Creek Massacre National Historic Study Site Act offered an official apology for an attack by U.S. soldiers on a Cheyenne village in Colorado. The attack occurred before the end of the Civil War in 1864.

Deciding Who Should Pay

Setting the issue of a statute of limitations aside, the fact remains that no former slaves or former slaveholders are still alive. This represents a problem. As Salzberger and Turck asked, "How are we to deal with old, even ancient injustices, when the current population contains neither the immediate victims nor the perpetrators?"[52] One answer to this question that may seem obvious is for the descendants of slaveholders to pay reparations to the descendants of slaves. This idea is not as simple as it sounds. The U.S. Census does not track descent from slaves or slave owners. It would be possible, of course, to use other historical records to determine who is descended from former slaveholders and seek reparations from them, but this approach has its problems. Since today's population is several generations removed from slavery, it is likely that many white people are descended from both slaveholders and abolitionists. Many people argue that descendants of white abolitionists and Union soldiers who fought to free the slaves should not be required to pay reparations.

Likewise, many people believe that recent immigrants, as well as descendants of immigrants who arrived in the United States after the Civil War ended, should not be required to share the financial burden of something that happened before they or their ancestors arrived in this country. However, van Dyke pointed out that "white people, speaking generally, continue to benefit from the burdens that were imposed for hundreds of years on Blacks. Even those whites whose ancestors immigrated to the United States after the Civil War benefit from the white skin privilege that still brings substantial benefits in our country."[53] Brooks agrees, arguing that when someone immigrates to a country, they must accept the positive as well as the negative aspects of that country. This means that U.S. immigrants can enjoy American freedoms but must also contribute to paying off a national debt that was incurred before they arrived. Brooks wrote, "Whether a recent arrival or a member of an old-line family, an inhabitant of a country cannot pick and choose from among aspects of the country's history. Certainly the nation's largest and longest moral debt, slavery carries over from generation to generation until it is paid off."[54]

Some people believe that the descendants of white Americans who fought in the Civil War or spoke out against segregation should contribute to paying reparations since they are all part of the United States. Van Dyke said,

> *Those whose ancestors participated in these noble initiatives, as well as those whose ancestors were not slave owners, may ask why they should now have to participate in reparations payments. They should not have to pay as individuals, of course, but it is still their country that authorized and sustained, through laws, courts, and police enforcement, an oppressive system that continues to stain our communities with discriminatory perceptions, beliefs, and practices. Because all white Americans benefit by being white, we all must participate in providing the economic compensation necessary to restore to the African Americans the property that was taken from them through the institution of slavery and its aftermath.*[55]

Asante agrees that because all white Americans, regardless of whether their ancestors did or did not own slaves, profit from belonging to the privileged race in the United States, all white Americans are responsible for paying reparations. He also pointed out that, in addition to insurance companies, railroad firms, and financial institutions, many American universities, including Harvard and Yale, have ties to the slave trade, which illustrates how pervasive the benefits of slavery were for whites.

Salzberger and Turck asked, "How, if at all, is responsibility for an injustice to be justly distributed among members of a group when some of those members were not themselves the causes of the deeds that cry out for remedy?"[56]

Robert K. Fullinwider, a philosopher, made an argument that if a nation owes a debt, then its citizens are required to

LOOKING TO HISTORY FOR GUIDANCE

Other examples of reparations paid by governments to groups of people for past wrongs could be used as models for a slavery reparations program. There are several examples around the world of reparations being made to a group of people.

One that seems particularly relevant is the case of the Japanese Americans who were forced into internment camps during World War II. The Civil Liberties Act of 1988 offered an official apology and $20,000 in reparations to each survivor or their surviving spouse or children. Another related example is the reparations paid by Germany to survivors of the Jewish Holocaust in World War II. The biggest difference between these two cases and that of reparations for slavery is that no former slaves are still alive. At the time of their reparations, direct victims of the Holocaust and the Japanese American internment were still living.

As David Horowitz wrote, in these and other cases, "the recipients of reparations were the direct victims of the injustice or their immediate families. This would be the only case of reparations to people who were not immediately affected and whose sole qualification to receive reparations would be racial."[1]

1. David Horowitz, *Uncivil Wars: The Controversy over Reparations for Slavery*. San Francisco, CA: Encounter, 2002, p. 13.

pay their share of that debt. The reparations for Japanese Americans, for example, were paid out of American taxpayer dollars. Fullinwider said, "One can make a parallel argument for reparations to African Americans ... Just as it was the nation that owed Japanese Americans reparations, so it is the nation that owes reparations to African Americans. And so it is that Americans not as individuals but as citizens owe support for the nation's debt."[57]

One approach would be to follow the example of German companies that were involved in slave labor during World War II. In 2001, these companies, as well as the German government, paid into a $5 billion fund established for the victims. The

In addition to formally apologizing for the internment of Japanese Americans during World War II, the U.S. government paid $20,000 to surviving victims or the families of those who had died.

amounts paid by each company varied according to the scope of each corporation's business activities. Van Dyke said, "Utilizing this approach, the Southern states and the federal government, plus those companies that benefited or profited from slavery, should contribute to the reparations fund."[58] Further, Brooks stated that because white Southerners actually fought to retain the institution of slavery, "white Southerners carry additional responsibility"[59] when it comes to payment of reparations.

Determining Who Should Benefit

Just as it is difficult to determine who should pay reparations for slavery, it is also difficult to determine who should receive reparations. The U.S. Census does not track descent from slaves, and accurate records of slaves themselves were not commonly kept. For example, many slaves did not have birth certificates or marriage certificates. The latter was mainly because marriage between slaves was not legally recognized. Families were often separated by masters who sold slaves to another owner, making the descendants of slaves difficult to trace. It would be easier to track the descendants of slaveholders. In addition, not every African American in the United States today is descended from slaves, so race alone would not be enough to determine eligibility for reparations. The difficulties involved in identifying the victims of slavery and discrimination create problems when it comes to determining who should be eligible for reparations. Fullinwider asked, "Should every individual black person receive reparations? Quite obviously, different blacks have fared very differently under past segregation. Most of those affected worst are long dead."[60]

Even if it could be agreed that reparations were due to every black American because of the effects of racial discrimination, some people raise questions about how to identify the recipients. Many Americans have a multiracial identity and do not identify as one single race. Opponents of reparations raise questions that seek to determine the eligibility of recipients of reparations. Neoconservative political commentator, writer, and critic of reparations David Frum asked, "[Do] recent immigrants from Africa or the West Indies [qualify]? What about future immigrants?"[61]

Some people believe that to be entitled to reparations for racial discrimination and segregation, a biracial person must have suffered the effects of discrimination and segregation. Proving that would be extremely complicated. In addition, there is little consensus about whether all black people should receive the same amount. Similarly, Fullinwider asked, "Do we pay the same to the child of middle class blacks who immigrated to the United States from the West Indies twenty years ago that we pay to an elderly retiree who spent half his life as a field hand in Mississippi?"[62]

The Cost of Reparations

Estimates of what it would cost to pay reparations for slavery range into the billions and even trillions of dollars. Some examples of dollar amounts that have been called for include Forman's

CONCERNS ABOUT REPARATIONS

Kimberley Jane Wilson is a conservative African American writer. Here, she echoes the concerns shared by many people over the complexities of reparations for slavery:

> *Will every black person who can prove he or she is a descendant of slaves get a check? Will we all get a tax credit? Will every black child get a scholarship to the college of their choice? How black do you have to be to get reparations? If one of your parents or grandparents is white, are you still eligible? ...*
>
> *Will we be getting reparations from Great Britain? After all, colonial America belonged to England when slavery was introduced here in 1619. Do Native Americans owe us reparations? Some tribes took an active part in owning slaves. In fact, there were even free blacks who purchased slaves. Do the descendants of these people owe reparations? ...*
>
> *No amount of apologies and no amount of cash can wash away the sin of slavery. Giving me a check as "compensation" for the agony of my ancestors trivializes their suffering. I feel uneasy at the thought of making a profit from that suffering.*[1]

1. Kimberley Jane Wilson, "Reparations, Anyone?," Project 21. www.nationalcenter.org/P21NVWilsonReparations801.html.

$500 million, while Boris Bittker reports the estimated present-day value of slave labor would be between $448 billion and $995 billion, and Farmer-Paellmann puts that figure at $1.4 trillion. Columnist Jonah Goldberg pointed out that some people call for $100,000 for a family of four, while others call for $100,000 for each individual; he estimates that "for a country that has at minimum 36.4 million people who call themselves black or African-American,"[63] the total amount might come to something around $3 trillion.

Georgetown professor Richard America, author of *Paying the Social Debt: What White America Owes Black America*, estimated the U.S. government owes African Americans $5 trillion to $10 trillion. University of Connecticut researcher Thomas Craemer determined that U.S. slave labor amounts to $5.9 trillion as of 2016. His amount only includes forced slave labor from 1815 to 1861 at an estimated 84 hours per week. Jack White, the grandson of a slave who has written for *TIME* magazine, accounted for more than just 47 years of unpaid hourly wages. He calculated that the amount owed for the unpaid wages of 10 million slaves for nearly 250 years, plus compensation for pain and suffering, with interest, amounts to $24 trillion.

The group N'COBRA believes that the amount must be completely dependent on African Americans' suffering and not on any historical acts of reparations:

> *Once we know how much damage has been done to us, and what is required to repair the damage, we will know how much is owed. We cannot allow anyone to offer, or accept on our behalf, some arbitrary figure based on some other peoples' reparations settlement. For example, the four year internment of Japanese in America, or the five year holocaust of Jewish people in Europe may require a different set of remedies than the 500 years holocaust of Africans in America. The nature and extent of the damage and the number of people impacted will dictate the type, duration, and amount of reparations owed. Some estimate $8 trillion.*[64]

Creating a Reparations Plan

Another difficulty in determining a program of reparations is the question of whether they should be made in the form of individual payments, as was done in the case of Japanese Americans, or in the form of increased funding for health care, education, and social programs. Many reparations activists favor the latter. Robinson proposes a trust fund for education, reparations from institutions that benefited from slavery, and continued advocacy for civil rights. Brooks proposes a museum of slavery as well. In 2017, at the direction of the Equal Justice Initiative, the From Enslavement to Mass Incarceration museum broke

WHITE'S SOLUTION FOR SLAVERY REPARATIONS

Slave descendant Jack White was a writer for *TIME* magazine who favors reparations for slavery. Instead of individual payouts, he believes that any funds paid as reparations should be put into social programs that would benefit African Americans. White wrote,

> *Use the money to uplift those who have been most hurt not only by the legacy of slavery but by existing discrimination and poverty: the urban and rural black poor. Put the money into a fund—call it the New Freedmen's Bureau—to finance the construction of schools, housing, transportation grids, factories, you name it, in the most depressed areas where the descendants of slaves are a majority. Use it to help finance new black-owned companies, to put poor black kids through college and endow cash-poor historically black universities, to run drug-treatment and job-training centers.*[1]

White estimated that the United States owes slave descendants $24 trillion. He said that this money, if used in the way he has described, would fight "present-day injustice and social ills instead of futilely trying to atone for the sins of the past"[2] by making individual payments to descendants of slaves.

1. Jack E. White, "Sorry Isn't Good Enough," *TIME*, June 30, 1997. www.time.com/time/magazine/article/0,9171,986599,00.html.

2. White, "Sorry Isn't Good Enough."

ground in Montgomery, Alabama.

Others have suggested funding for job programs and housing, incentives to banks to give business loans to African Americans, scholarships, and educating all Americans about the history of African Americans. Asante sees the first step toward reparations as an official apology for slavery. He said, "To apologize is noble; not to apologize, in the light of the horrors of enslavement, segregation, and continuing discrimination, is arrogant."[65]

Asante further stated that,

while the cost of reparations for slavery will be huge, reparations do not need to be in the form of individual monetary payouts:

> *Although it will cost billions of dollars, it will not have to be the doling out of billions of dollars of cash to individuals. While the delivery of money ... is different from most other reparations agreements, it is possible for reparations to be advanced in the United States by a number of other means. Among the potential options are educational, health care, land or property grants, and a combination of such grants. Any reparation remedy should deal with long-term issues in the African American community rather than a one-time cash payout.*[66]

Another question is what exactly reparations for slavery would be for. As van Dyke asked, "Because those who were actual slaves are now dead, do their heirs have a continuing right to compensation? Is that right to compensation based on the wrong done to the ancestors, or to the continuing effects of that wrong that burden the descendants today, or both?"[67] The answers to these questions have a direct bearing on how much should be paid, in what form, and to whom. Unfortunately, there are no clear-cut answers to most of these questions.

CHAPTER FIVE

THE CONTROVERSY OVER REPARATIONS

Reparations for slavery is a widely debated topic. There are many schools of thought about whether they are necessary or even a good idea. Some feel that making reparations might worsen the racial divide and increase the mentality of white superiority. There is also the issue of constitutionality.

Of course, many people oppose these ideas and see the need for and potential benefits of reparations. However, when and how these reparations take place may not be determined soon, if ever, because of the issue's controversial nature.

A Radical Perspective

Conservative American author David Horowitz boldly and vocally opposes reparations. In 2001, he harshly criticized reparations in an essay titled "Ten Reasons Why Reparations for Slavery Is a Bad Idea—and Racist Too" in U.S. college newspapers. Horowitz presented highly offensive ideas, such as that African Americans benefited from slavery by being brought from Africa to the more prosperous United States. He stated, "The claim for reparations is premised on the false assumption that only whites have benefited from slavery."[68] Horowitz continued his controversial argument: "America's African American citizens are the richest and most privileged black people alive—a bounty that is a direct result of the heritage [of slavery and its abolition] that is under assault."[69]

The essay, written by the white author, ignited a huge controversy. Horowitz is not alone in his views, though. Ward Connerly, a black conservative public figure, and Dinesh D'Souza, an Indian American conservative author and public commentator, both publicly agreed with Horowitz—so did black conservative economist and

HOROWITZ'S OPPOSITION TO REPARATIONS

Deemed highly controversial and offensive to many people at the time it was published, David Horowitz's "Ten Reasons Why Reparations for Slavery Is a Bad Idea—and Racist Too" outlines his argument:

1. *There Is No Single Group Clearly Responsible For The Crime Of Slavery*
2. *There Is No One Group That Benefited Exclusively From Its Fruits*
3. *Only A Tiny Minority Of White Americans Ever Owned Slaves, And Others Gave Their Lives To Free Them*
4. *America Today Is A Multi-Ethnic Nation and Most Americans Have No Connection (Direct Or Indirect) To Slavery*
5. *The Historical Precedents Used To Justify The Reparations Claim Do Not Apply, And The Claim Itself Is Based On Race Not Injury*
6. *The Reparations Argument Is Based On The Unfounded Claim That All African-American Descendants of Slaves Suffer From The Economic Consequences Of Slavery And Discrimination*
7. *The Reparations Claim Is One More Attempt To Turn African-Americans Into Victims. It Sends A Damaging Message To The African-American Community.*
8. *Reparations To African Americans Have Already Been Paid*
9. *What About The Debt Blacks Owe To America?*
10. *The Reparations Claim Is A Separatist Idea That Sets African-Americans Against The Nation That Gave Them Freedom*[1]

1. David Horowitz, *Uncivil Wars: The Controversy over Reparations for Slavery*. San Francisco, CA: Encounter, 2002, pp. 12–15.

author Thomas Sowell, who asked, "Does anyone seriously suggest that blacks in America today would be better off if they were in Africa?"[70] Even the prominent African American leader Booker T. Washington, who was born into slavery, wrote in his 1901 autobiography, *Up from Slavery*,

> *The 10 million Negroes inhabiting this country, who themselves or whose ancestors went through the school of American slavery, are in a stronger and more hopeful condition, materially, intellectually, morally, and religiously, than is true of an equal number of black people in any other portion of the globe.*[71]

Paying for An Ancestor's Sins

Some people believe that requiring Americans today to contribute to the bill for slave reparations is unfair. Steve Dasbach, the former executive director of the Libertarian Party, said, "No one alive today had anything to do with the morally repugnant policy of slavery. So confiscating their money for reparations amounts to punishing people for crimes committed by someone else—more than 100 years ago."[72] Philosopher and author Janna Thompson explained this point of view further:

> *Requiring that presently existing people make reparation for injustices done by their predecessors seems to many people to be not all that different from punishing people for crimes they did not commit.*[73]

Robinson argued that reparations for slavery are still justified today. He described slavery as "a human rights crime without parallel in the modern world" and said "it produces its victims *ad infinitum* [without end], long after the active stage of the crime has ended."[74]

Slavery's continuing legacy of racial discrimination leaves many to agree that black Americans are entitled to reparations. Slavery inhibited African Americans from acquiring wealth, land, and education that they could have passed down to their families. This is often cited as the main reason for income and racial inequality in America.

Thompson argued that members of a nation do have historical obligations and a duty to repair past wrongs. She said, "The fact that our predecessors or forebears were the ones who did the wrongs does not excuse us from a responsibility for reparation."[75] This view is commonly held throughout the world, as van Dyke explained:

> *The world has long recognized the enslavement of one person by another as one of the grossest*

AMERICANS' THOUGHTS ON REPARATIONS

YouGov, a market research firm, explored the opinions about reparations and discrimination of both white and black Americans. Their research in 2014 showed a substantial difference of opinion along racial lines. When asked about reparations, only 19 percent of white individuals supported education and job training programs, compared to 63 percent of black individuals. Only 6 percent of white individuals thought the government should offer cash payments, while 59 percent of black individuals were in favor. In total, only 15 percent of the public are in favor of any form of reparations.

Opinions among both races changed significantly when participants were asked what they would have thought if reparations had been made directly to former slaves. In total, 37 percent would have been in favor, and only 31 percent opposed. This suggests that many feel today's citizens are too far removed from slavery to receive reparations.

YouGov's study also found that 51 percent of white individuals did not believe that slavery's legacy has had any financial impact on African Americans' lower than average wealth levels. When black individuals were asked the same question, 48 percent said that slavery is a major factor. These numbers alone showed once again why reparations for slavery is such a complex issue.

violations of the fundamental human rights of individuals. The international community has also reached a solid consensus that all violations of human rights must be investigated and documented, that the perpetrators of human rights abuses must be punished, and that the victims of human rights violations have a right to compensation.[76]

The late civil rights activist Malcolm X explained his views on why paying reparations today for something done by one's ancestors is the right thing to do: "If you are the son of a man who had a wealthy estate and you inherit your father's estate, you have to pay off the debts that your father incurred before he died ... Your father isn't here to pay. My father isn't here to collect. But

I'm here to collect and you're here to pay."[77]

A Chance of Worsened Race Relations

Some groups and individuals believe that paying reparations for slavery could increase racism. Dasbach said, "Forcing people who had nothing to do with slavery to pay others who were never enslaved is the height of injustice and will only exacerbate racial tension in America." He added, "Millions of white Americans who have no reason to dislike blacks may find one the moment they're forced to pay a race tax."[78] Another critic pointed to the anger that Germans felt over the vast war reparations their country was forced to pay after World War I and said, "Reparations can be dangerous ... Reparations breed envy and distrust and stir up hatred."[79]

Bittker agrees that reparations would increase racism but for a different reason. In his book *The Case for Black Reparations*, he explained that any reparations payments that are based on race will, by necessity, require official definitions and classifications of race in order to determine eligibility. Bittker wrote,

> *I venture to predict that the adoption of a formal code of racial classification ... would have calamitous consequences for the United States ... It would put pressure on millions of persons of mixed blood to make an official declaration of their racial origin.*[80]

Some opponents of reparations argue that reparations would increase racism by implying that African Americans need extra help in order to compete with whites. Author John McWhorter described the racial harm he believes reparations to slave descendants would create in the United States:

> *There would be damage on both sides of the racial divide. As the magic transformations of the package inevitably failed to appear, the flop would be attributed to there not having been enough money granted. Next a new mantra would become established in the black community to cover the bitter disappointment: "They think they can treat us like animals for 400 years and then just pay us off?" Meanwhile, non-blacks would begin to grouse "They got reparations—what are they still complaining about?" Whether these mutterings would be valid is*

beside the point, what matters is that they would arise and be passed on to a new generation, to further poison inter-racial relations in this country.[81]

The Potential for Victimhood

Other critics argue that reparations would not only imply blacks need extra help but would also reinforce the role of blacks being victims. Horowitz wrote, "To focus the social passions of African Americans on what some Americans may have done to their ancestors 50 or 150 years ago is to burden them with a crippling sense of victimhood."[82] Connerly agreed, saying, "We don't want young black kids to grow up thinking they are weak and can't look after themselves."[83]

African American political commentator and nationally syndicated television and radio show host Armstrong Williams believes the reparations movement encourages the view of black people as inferior and is damaging to black people. He said,

> *As an American black, I find this stereotype of failure not only to be personally insulting, but also to be radically destabilizing. Simply to regard all members of a group as victims neatly removes such terms as "character" and "personal responsibility" from the cultural dialogue. After all, what need is there for individual striving when it is plainly understood that all the difficulties that blacks suffer are the direct indisputable result of incidents that occurred centuries ago. The real danger of reparations, then, is that it presumes that being black is synonymous with being inferior. By extension, all blacks are encouraged to identify themselves as victims, even those who are plainly among society's privileged.*[84]

Nothing Will Compensate for Slavery

Some believe that money can never make up for the situation African Americans were forced into during the slavery era and beyond. Van Dyke agreed with this view and said, "The final figure should indeed be very large, to give everyone involved a sense of honest closure, but ... it will never be large enough to provide a true level of compensation for the losses that were suffered by so many generations of African Americans."[85] Still other people believe that any offer of money would be an insult to African Americans.

Attorney Richard Lichtman wrote,

> *The Negro's past suffering seems beyond the remedy of society to redeem. There is no payment that can supply its balance. It would be a sign of contempt for the Negro should the white community offer to compensate this debt ... The strictly compensatory act of payment for past suffering is impossible.*[86]

Was the Debt Already Paid?

Other opponents of the reparations movement claim that African Americans have already been compensated for slavery. Former Speaker of the House Newt Gingrich, columnist George F. Will, conservative writer and editor Terence P. Jeffery, and others believe that the debt for slavery was paid with the lives of those who fought to end the practice.

Critics of this argument point to the fact that the Civil War was not fought expressly to end slavery but rather to save the Union. They also point out that the Civil War did not end the mistreatment of African Americans in the United States. Even after slavery was abolished, black Americans continued to exist in a state of near-bondage for another century. As Brooks explained, "Ending slavery only to impose another, albeit less severe, system of racial subordination on blacks is more akin to a slap in the face than an apology or reparations for slavery."[87]

The reforms of the 1960s, including Johnson's Great Society, civil rights legislation, and the policy of affirmative action, are cited as further examples of ways in which restitution for slavery has already been paid. Horowitz wrote,

> *Since the passage of the Civil Rights Acts and the advent of the Great Society in 1965, trillions of dollars in transfer payments have been made to African Americans in the form of welfare benefits and racial preferences (in contracts, job placements and educational admissions)—all under the rationale of redressing historic racial grievances. It is said that reparations are necessary to achieve a healing between African Americans and other Americans. If trillion-dollar restitutions and a wholesale rewriting of American law (in order to accommodate racial preferences) is not enough to achieve a "healing," what is?*[88]

Some scholars have suggested that reparations for slavery were already paid by the lives lost during the American Civil War.

Reparations activists counter that because civil rights laws and affirmative action apply to more than just African Americans, these reforms cannot substitute for true reparations for slavery. In addition, African Americans have not received an official apology from the United States government or an admission of responsibility for slavery and its legacy.

Slavery's Legal Status

If slavery was legal when it was practiced, was anyone actually breaking the law?

Many opponents of reparations feel the answer to this question is "no" because slavery was a universally acceptable practice at the time it occurred in the United States. Other nations around the world and throughout history practiced slavery, as far back as ancient Mesopotamia. Therefore, some argue that it would not be fair to condemn the U.S. government for something that was not seen as wrong at the time.

However, as Brooks said, by the time of the American Revolution, most of the Western world no longer approved of slavery or viewed it a moral practice. Furthermore, Brooks wrote, "The American colonists were certainly aware of the changing global perspective on slavery, but they chose to ignore it." With the notable exception of Benjamin Franklin, many of America's Founding Fathers and writers of the Declaration of Independence and Constitution were slaveholders, as were eight of the first twelve U.S. presidents. The government even forced slaves to rebuild

President Thomas Jefferson owned slaves at his home, Monticello; the property is now a tourist attraction where visitors can learn more about Jefferson's slaves.

the White House following damage during the War of 1812. These facts, Brooks argued, provide a rational basis for the government to compensate African Americans for the effects of slavery: "Clearly, then, American slavery was different. It kept alive a moribund [declining] institution—one that Western societies had marked for extinction due to its moral bankruptcy."[89]

Opponents of reparations argue in turn that since slavery was legal at the time it was practiced in the United States, there is technically no ground to seek restitutions for slavery from the U.S. government, especially because the U.S. Constitution forbids

what are known as ex post facto, or retroactive, laws that criminalize actions that were legal at the time they occurred.

In addition, the legal principle of sovereign immunity makes it very difficult to seek reparations from the government at all. Sovereign immunity means that nations, or sovereigns, are exempt from lawsuits by private citizens. In the United States, as in other countries, the federal government cannot be sued without its permission. However, reparations activists point out that the government can, and often does, waive sovereign immunity and consent to being sued. In fact, some say that the right to claim sovereign immunity has already been waived. Crimes against humanity, such as slavery and the transatlantic slave trade, are not entitled to sovereign immunity protections. This gives reparations activists hope that a successful lawsuit can be brought against the United States in the future.

What Does the Future Hold?

What is the future of slavery reparations? As more time separates the United States from the abolition of slavery 150 years ago, the answer to this question will only become more complicated. In 2016, President Obama spoke to these complications when he said, "So the bottom line is that it's hard to find a model in which you can practically administer and sustain political support for those kinds of efforts (reparations). And what makes America complicated as well is the degree to which this is not just a black/white society, and it is becoming less so every year."[90]

American journalist Ta-Nehisi Coates feels that the complications go far deeper than just America's racial makeup. He wrote, "we stand to discover much about ourselves in such a discussion (about reparations)—and that is perhaps what scares us. The idea of reparations is frightening not simply because we might lack the ability to pay. The idea of reparations threatens something much deeper—America's heritage, history, and standing in the world."[91]

Addressing Obama's and Coates's

THE UNITED NATIONS WEIGHS IN

In 1962, African American civil rights leader Audley Moore petitioned the United Nations (UN) to demand the United States pay reparations for slavery. Her goal became a reality in 2016, more than 50 years after her petition was submitted. The United Nations Working Group of Experts on People of African Descent spent 14 years and 20 days interviewing federal, state, and local departments; families who lost their children to racial violence; descendants of slaves; and civil rights activists. Their research resulted in a firm recommendation that the United States create a plan to make reparations for slavery.

Audley Moore once considered moving to Africa with Marcus Garvey's organization but instead remained in the United States where she fought for African American civil rights.

The chairperson of the group, Ricardo Sunga, wrote, "The group urges a serious consideration of a full formal apology, repatriation, cultural institutions, public health initiatives, African knowledge programs, psychological rehabilitation, technological transfer, and debt cancellation."[1] Amongst many other recommendations was one asking Congress to pass H.R. 40, the Commission to Study Reparation Proposals for African Americans Act.

The UN's efforts are a huge step toward slavery reparations becoming a reality in the United States.

1. Quoted in Pamela Falk, "Should U.S. Pay Reparations for Slavery? U.N.-appointed Experts Think So," CBS News, September 27, 2016. www.cbsnews.com/news/should-us-pay-reparations-for-slavery-united-nations-working-groups-think-so/.

concerns will require both time and government initiative. In the interim, many believe there is hope for a future America where racial tensions and discrimination are a thing of the past. Although not a solution to slavery reparations, it would be a step in the right direction. Obama has seen changes during his lifetime that give him this hope. In an interview with Coates, he said,

> *I do believe America has changed ... The majority of Americans believe in the idea of nondiscrimination. They believe in the idea that Jamal and Johnny should be treated equally. They believe in the idea that a child shouldn't be consigned to poverty just because of circumstances of their birth. Now, in practice, in daily social interactions, etc., there may be all kinds of biases and prejudices that are unspoken, that people aren't aware of, that affect who's hired, and who gets loans, and how kids are treated in school. But it's a powerful thing if you have on your side an idea (nondiscrimination) that the overwhelming majority of people believe in because that's how you can build a consensus that's lasting.*[92]

An attitude of nondiscrimination held by the majority of citizens can carry America forward toward healing, even if widespread government reparations for slavery never occur.

The Equal Justice Initiative also believes that education and preserving history will help with healing racial tensions and past hurts. It is focused on telling the story of racially motivated lynching in America by erecting a memorial in Montgomery, Alabama, featuring the names of more than 4,000 lynching victims. Beside it will sit a museum that tells the history of slavery and its aftermath. This is how the organization is raising awareness of the way African Americans were treated during slavery.

Although a large-scale, government-led plan for slavery reparations has yet to be enacted, the slavery reparations movement has had wins in recent years. Many U.S. states and companies have apologized for their role in slavery and the ways in which they benefited from it. Georgetown University is now offering preferential admissions to descendants of slaves as a way to make up for how the institution benefited from slavery. The U.S. Senate and House apologized for the Jim Crow laws and slavery with bills in 2007 and 2009. In 2017, many states and cities removed or relocated Confederate statues that

From Charlottesville to the White House:
Shut down white supremacy!
PSLweb.org
RACISM KILLS

haunted many of those affected by slavery. Most notably, after 14 years of research, the United Nations officially asked the United States in 2016 to act on slavery reparations and pass H.R. 40.

Slavery reparations opponents still remain vocal, and reparations for slavery still remains a controversial issue for many. Obama's and Coates's concerns are still very real. Acts of racial violence and discrimination continue to penetrate American society. However, hope is not lost because the slavery reparations movement is still gaining momentum even 150 years after the abolition of slavery. The future of slavery reparations may still be unknown, but those who support reparations have reasons to believe they will become a reality.

Many people want all Confederate memorials in the United States torn down because they feel these memorials honor those who enslaved African Americans.

NOTES

Introduction: Slavery's Effect on America

1. Molefi Kete Asante, *Erasing Racism: The Survival of the American Nation*. Amherst, NY: Prometheus, 2003, p. 246.

2. John David Smith, *Black Voices from Reconstruction, 1865–1877*. Gainesville, FL: University Press of Florida, 1997, p. 152.

3. Quoted in Bill Chappell, "'We Are Not Cured': Obama Discusses Racism in America with Marc Maron," NPR, June 22, 2015. www.npr.org/sections/thetwo-way/2015/06/22/416476377/we-are-not-cured-obama-discusses-racism-in-america-with-marc-maron.

4. Roy L. Brooks, *Atonement and Forgiveness: A New Model for Black Reparations*. Oakland, CA: University of California Press, 2006, p. 8.

Chapter One: Defining Slavery Reparations

5. "What Is Reparations?," National Coalition of Blacks for Reparations in America (N'COBRA), 2017. www.ncobra.org/aboutus.htm.

6. Brooks, *Atonement and Forgiveness*, p. 20.

7. Brooks, *Atonement and Forgiveness*, pp. 187–188.

8. Quoted in Brooks, *Atonement and Forgiveness*, p. 185.

9. Asante, *Erasing Racism*, p. 263.

10. Quoted in Randall Robinson, *The Debt: What America Owes to Blacks*. New York, NY: Dutton, 2000, p. 226.

11. Len Cooper, "Slavery Did Not End with the Civil War," Len Cooper's Village, June 16, 1996. www.greatlinx.com/peonage.htm.

12. Lisa Delpit, *Other People's Children: Cultural Conflict in the Classroom*. New York, NY: New Press, 1995, p. 92.

13. Asante, *Erasing Racism*, p. 186.

14. Asante, *Erasing Racism*, p. 8.

15. Robinson, *The Debt*, p. 8.

Chapter Two: First Attempts at Reparations

16. Quoted in Roy L. Brooks, ed., *When Sorry Isn't Enough: The Controversy over Apologies and Reparations for Human Injustice*. New York, NY: New York University Press, 1999, p. 365.

17. Quoted in Brooks, *Atonement and Forgiveness*, p. 120.

18. Quoted in Raymond A. Winbush, *Should America Pay?: Slavery and the Raging Debate on Reparations*. New York, NY: Amistad, 2003, p. 15.

19. Mary Frances Berry, *My Face Is Black Is True: Callie House and the Struggle for Ex-Slave Reparations*. New York, NY: Knopf, 2005, p. 12.

20. Berry, *My Face Is Black Is True*, p. 11.

21. Ronald Paul Salzberger and Mary C. Turck, ed., *Reparations for Slavery: A Reader*. Lanham, MD: Rowman & Littlefield Publishers, 2004, p. 67.

22. Gerene L. Freeman, "What About My 40 Acres and a Mule?," Yale-New Haven Teachers Institute, 1994. www.yale.edu/ynhti/curriculum/units/1994/4/94.04.01.x.html#b.

23. Quoted in Berry, *My Face Is Black Is True*, p. 73.

24. Quoted in Berry, *My Face Is Black Is True*, p. 50.

25. Quoted in Berry, *My Face Is Black Is True*, p. 39.

26. Quoted in Berry, *My Face Is Black Is True*, p. 180.

27. Berry, *My Face Is Black Is True*, p. 182.

28. Quoted in Winbush, *Should America Pay?*, p. 27.

29. Quoted in Berry, *My Face Is Black Is True*, p. 223.

30. Quoted in Berry, *My Face Is Black Is True*, p. 224.

Chapter Three: Reparations from the 1960s to Today

31. Quoted in Marcus Epstein, "Myths of Martin Luther King," LewRockwell.com, January 18, 2003. www.lewrockwell.com/orig/epstein 9.html.

32. Quoted in "In the News," Millions for Reparations. www.millionsforreparations.com.

33. Quoted in Robert Mann, *The Walls of Jericho: Lyndon Johnson, Hubert Humphrey, Richard Russell, and the Struggle for Civil Rights*. New York, NY: Mariner, 1997, p. 503.

34. Quoted in Lyndon Baines Johnson Library and Museum, "President Lyndon B. Johnson's Commencement Address at Howard University: 'To Fulfill These Rights.'" www.lbjlib.utexas.edu/johnson/archives.hom/speeches.hom/650604.asp.

35. Quoted in Boris I. Bittker, *The Case for Black Reparations*. Boston, MA: Beacon, 2003, p. 161.

36. Quoted in Bittker, *The Case for Black Reparations*, p. 167.

37. Quoted in Bittker, *The Case for Black Reparations*, p. 168.

38. Quoted in Bittker, *The Case for Black Reparations*, p. 27.

39. Quoted in Salzberger and Turck, *Reparations for Slavery*, p. 75.

40. Quoted in Mary Frances Berry and John W. Blassingame, *Long Memory: The Black Experience in America*. New York, NY: Oxford Univeristy Press, 1982, p. 406.

41. John Conyers Jr., "Major Issues—Reparations," Congressman John Conyers Jr. www.house.gov/ conyers/news_reparations.htm.

42. Quoted in Salzberger and Turck, *Reparations for Slavery*, p. 91.

43. Quoted in Congressman Tony P. Hall, "Hall Calls on Congress to Apologize for Slavery," June 19,

2000. www.directblackaction.com/tony_hall.htm.

44. Quoted in Peter Viles, "Suit Seeks Billions in Slave Reparations," CNN, March 27, 2002. archives.cnn.com/2002/LAW/03/2 6/slavery.reparations.

45. Deadria Farmer-Paellmann, "Personal Testimony of Deadria Farmer-Paellmann in Support of H. R. 40—Commission to Study Reparations Proposals for African Americans Act," National Coalition of Blacks for Reparations in America (N'COBRA). www.ncobra.org/pdffiles/DEADRIA%20april%206%20statement.pdf.

46. Quoted in Larry O'Dell, "Virginia Lawmakers Pass Slavery Apology," Associated Press, February 24, 2007. news.aol.com/topnews/articles/_a/virginia-lawmakers-pass-slavery-apology/20070224211409990002?ncid=NWS00010000000001.

47. "A Concurrent Resolution Apologizing for the Enslavement and Racial Segregation of African Americans, Con. Res. 26, 111 Cong," June 18, 2009. www.govtrack.us/congress/bills/111/sconres26/text/es.

Chapter Four: The Reality of Reparations

48. Quoted in Winbush, *Should America Pay?*, p. 73.

49. Quoted in Winbush, *Should America Pay?*, p. 76.

50. Quoted in Winbush, *Should America Pay?*, p. 58.

51. Suzette M. Malveaux, "Statutes of Limitations: A Policy Analysis in the Context of Reparations Litigation," 74 George Washington Law Review, November 2005.

52. Salzberger and Turck, *Reparations for Slavery*, p. xii.

53. Quoted in Winbush, *Should America Pay?*, pp. 72–73.

54. Brooks, *Atonement and Forgiveness*, p. 190.

55. Quoted in Winbush, *Should America Pay?*, p. 75.

56. Salzberger and Turck, *Reparations for Slavery*, p. xii.

57. Quoted in Salzberger and Turck, *Reparations for Slavery*, p. 143.

58. Quoted in Winbush, *Should America Pay?*, p. 73.

59. Brooks, *Atonement and Forgiveness*, p. 190.

60. Quoted in Salzberger and Turck, *Reparations for Slavery*, p. 148.

61. David Frum, "The Impossibility of Reparations," *The Atlantic*, June 3, 2014. www.theatlantic.com/business/archive/2014/06/the-impossibility-of-reparations/372041/.62.

62. Quoted in Salzberger and Turck, *Reparations for Slavery*, p. 148.

63. Jonah Goldberg, "Reparations Now," *National Review Online*, March 19, 2001. www.national review.com/goldberg/goldbergprint 031901.html.

64. "How Much Is Owed?," N'COBRA. www.ncobra.com/ncobra_info.htm.

65. Asante, *Erasing Racism*, p. 236.

66. Asante, *Erasing Racism*, p. 264.

67. Quoted in Winbush, *Should America Pay?*, p. 58.

Chapter Five: The Controversy Over Reparations

68. David Horowitz, *Uncivil Wars: The Controversy over Reparations for Slavery*. San Francisco, CA: Encounter, 2002, p. 12.

69. Horowitz, *Uncivil Wars*, pp. 15–16.

70. Quoted in Horowitz, *Uncivil Wars*, p. 130.

71. Booker T. Washington, *Up from Slavery*. New York, NY: Doubleday, 1901, e-book.

72. Quoted in "Libertarian Party Press Release: Slavery Reparations," Chuckhawks.com, August 20, 2002. www. chuckhawks.com/lprelease_slavery_reparations.htm.

73. Janna Thompson, *Taking Responsibility for the Past: Reparation and Historical*

Injustice. Malden, MA: Blackwell Publishers Inc., 2002, p. xii.

74. Robinson, *The Debt*, p. 216.

75. Thompson, *Taking Responsibility for the Past*, p. xviii.

76. Quoted in Winbush, *Should America Pay?*, p. 57.

77. Quoted in "In the News," Millions for Reparations.

78. Quoted in "Libertarian Party Press Release: Slavery Reparations," Chuckhawks.com.

79. Quoted in Salzberger and Turck, *Reparations for Slavery*, p. 99.

80. Bittker, *The Case for Black Reparations*, p. 97.

81. John McWhorter, "Blood Money," *American Enterprise*, July/August 2001. www.taemag.com/issues/ articleid.15514/article_detail.asp.

82. Quoted in Salzberger and Turck, *Reparations for Slavery*, p. 129.

83. Quoted in Brooks, *Atonement and Forgiveness*, p. 41.

84. Quoted in Winbush, *Should America Pay?*, p. 167.

85. Quoted in Winbush, *Should America Pay?*, p. 74.

86. Quoted in Salzberger and Turck, *Reparations for Slavery*, p. 90.

87. Brooks, *Atonement and Forgiveness*, p. 194.

88. Horowitz, *Uncivil Wars*, p. 14.

89. Brooks, *Atonement and Forgiveness*, p. 187.

90. Quoted in Ta-Nehisi Coates, "'Better Is Good': Obama on Reparations, Civil Rights, and the Art of the Possible," *The Atlantic*, December 21, 2016. www.theatlantic.com/politics/archive/2016/12/ta-nehisi-coates-obama-transcript-ii/511133/.

91. Ta-Nehisi Coates, "The Case for Reparations," *The Atlantic*, June 2014. www.theatlantic.com/magazine/archive/2014/06/the-case-for-reparations/361631/.

92. Quoted in Ta-Nehisi Coates, "'Better Is Good.'"

FOR MORE INFORMATION

Books

Asante, Molefi Kete. *Erasing Racism: The Survival of the American Nation*. 2nd ed. Buffalo, NY: Prometheus Books, 2016.
Asante writes about the discrimination that African Americans continue to face even though many whites believe racism no longer exists in America.

Asare, William Kweku. *Slavery Reparations in Perspective*. Victoria, BC: Trafford, 2002.
In this book, the author discusses the necessity of dealing with the issues of the transatlantic slave trade, slavery, and reparations.

Berry, Mary Frances. *My Face Is Black Is True: Callie House and the Struggle for Ex-Slave Reparations*. New York, NY: Knopf, 2005.
This book traces the efforts of Callie House to obtain pensions for former slaves in the early part of the 20th century.

Brophy, Alfred L. *Reparations Pro and Con*. New York, NY: Oxford University Press, 2006.
This book covers both sides of the debate over reparations for slavery.

Glaude, Eddie S. Jr. *Democracy in Black: How Race Still Enslaves the American Soul*. New York, NY: Crown, 2016.
Glaude writes about the race problem in modern America, including recent racially motivated acts of violence and the current political atmosphere.

Holland, Jesse. *The Invisibles: The Untold Story of African American Slaves in the White House*. Guilford, CT: Lyons Press, 2016.
This book shares the stories of slaves who worked for U.S. presidents and their staff in the White House.

Torpey, John. *Making Whole What Has Been Smashed: On Reparations Politics*. Cambridge, MA: Harvard University Press, 2006.
In this book, Torpey explains the politics of the global reparations movement.

Websites

Civil Rights and Restorative Justice Project (CRRJ) (nuweb9.neu.edu/civilrights)
Part of Northeastern University, the CRRJ provides information and resources for those seeking justice for crimes that took place during the civil rights period.

Equal Justice Initiative (EJI) (eji.org)
The Equal Justice Initiative wants to further social justice, protect everyone's human rights, and bring about reform in the U.S. criminal justice system.

N'COBRA (The National Coalition of Blacks for Reparations in America) (www.ncobraonline.org)
Founded in 1987, this group works to obtain reparations for African American slave descendants.

Thomas Jefferson's Monticello (monticello.org/site/plantation-and-slavery)
On this website, you'll find information about slavery and plantation life at Monticello, Thomas Jefferson's home.

"We Absolutely Could Give Reparations to Black People. Here's How" (www.huffingtonpost.com/entry/reparations-black-americans-slavery_us_56c4dfa9e4b08ffac1276bd7us_56c4dfa9e4b08ffac1276bd7)
This article provides in-depth information on how reparations for slavery could be provided.

INDEX

J

K

L

M

N

O

P

PICTURE CREDITS

Cover Mario Tama/Staff/Getty Images News/Getty Images; pp. 6 (top left), 11, 18, 26, 37 Bettmann/Contributor/Bettmann/Getty Images; p. 6 (top right) © North Wind Picture Archives; p. 6 (bottom) Ed Vebell/Contributor/Archive Photos/Getty Images; p. 7 (left) George Tames/Contributor/Archive Photos/Getty Images; p. 7 (right) Aaron Alex/Alamy Stock Photo; p. 9 ROBYN BECK/Staff/AFP/Getty Images; p. 10 a katz/Shutterstock.com; pp. 16–17 Universal History Archive/Contributor/Universal Images Group/Getty Images; p. 20 Everett Historical/Shutterstock.com; p. 21 Tom Williams/Contributor/CQ-Roll Call Group/Getty Images; pp. 23, 34, 49 Courtesy of the Library of Congress; p. 25 Library of Congress/Contributor/Corbis Historical/Getty Images; p. 28 Cincinnati Museum Center/Contributor/Archive Photos/Getty Images; p. 29 JEFF KOWALSKY/Stringer/AFP/Getty Images; p. 32 Jose Luis Vega/Shutterstock.com; p. 33 Rainer Lesniewski/Shutterstock.com; p. 40 Librariabryan/Wikimedia Commons; p. 47 Life Atlas Photography/Shutterstock.com; p. 48 914 collection/Alamy Stock Photo; p. 53 Photo 12/Contributor/Universal Images Group/Getty Images; p. 54 Charles Bonnay/Contributor/The LIFE Images Collection/Getty Images; pp. 58–59 AP Photo/Stephen Chernin; pp. 60–61 Van Payne UPI Photo Service/Newscom; p. 64 Rob Hainer/Shutterstock.com; p. 69 Eliot Elisofon/Contributor/The LIFE Picture Collection/Getty Images; pp. 82–83 Archive Photos/Stringer/Archive Photos/Getty Images; pp. 84–85 Tony Craddock/Shutterstock.com; p. 86 Schlesinger Library, Radcliffe Institute, Harvard University; p. 88–89 ZACH GIBSON/Contributor/AFP/Getty Images.

ABOUT THE AUTHOR

Sarah Goldy-Brown is a freelance writer and editor from Zionsville, PA. She holds a Bachelor of Arts degree in public relations from Messiah College. Sarah loves writing in all styles but currently specializes in e-commerce and other nonfiction content. This is her second book for Lucent Press.